PORTLAND
CONFIDENTIAL

PORTLAND
CONFIDENTIAL

SEX, CRIME, AND CORRUPTION IN THE ROSE CITY

PHIL STANFORD

ptown books

Sixth printing 2010

ptown books

2940 SE Berkeley Place
Portland OR 97202
503-786-7090
Visit ptownbooks.com

Originally published by Graphic Arts Center Publishing Company in 2004.

Editor: Tim Frew
Copy Editor: Kathy Howard
Photo Editor: Thomas Robinson, Historic Photo Archive
Designer: Elizabeth M. Watson, Watson Graphics

Cover design by Elizabeth Watson.
Photo credits are listed on page 190.

Library of Congress Catalogue Number 2004001009

ISBN 978-0-98289-581-8

Printed in the United States of America

For the good people of Portland,

especially Margaret.

CONTENTS

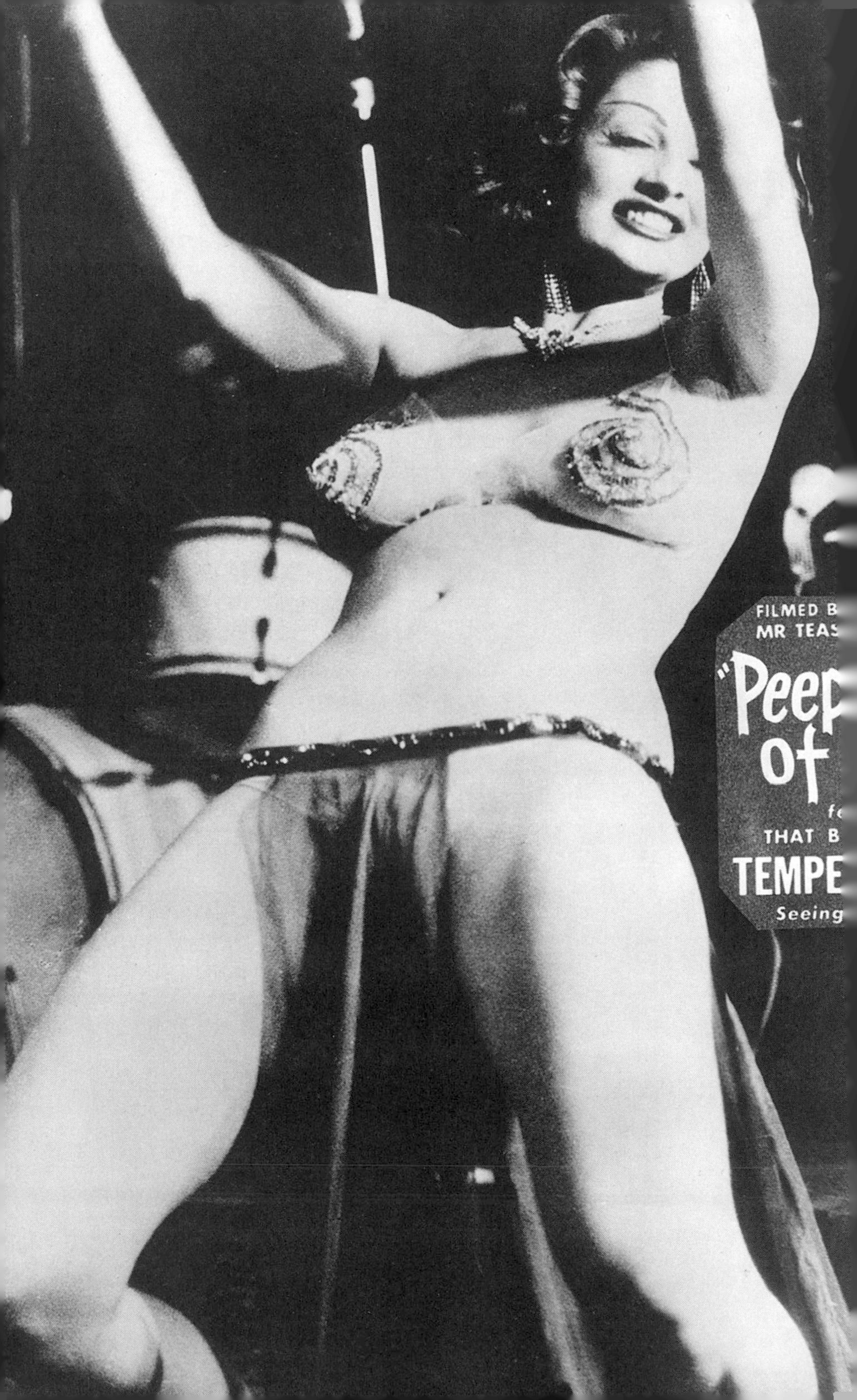
FILMED B
MR TEAS
"Peep
of
fe
THAT B
TEMPE
Seeing

PORTLAND'S BIGGEST DIRTY LITTLE SECRET

IT MAY COME AS A BIT OF A SHOCK, especially to anyone who has come to regard Portland as a haven for enlightened progressive thought, light rail, and lattes for all, that not too long ago—in fact, at least as recently as the 1950s—Portland was known throughout the country as a Mecca of vice and sin. If you were looking for a good time, or maybe a little bit more, Portland was the place to go on the West Coast.

> AS RECENTLY AS THE 1950S, PORTLAND WAS KNOWN THROUGHOUT THE COUNTRY AS A MECCA OF VICE AND SIN.

It was a wide-open town, with purveyors of all the traditional vices operating openly under the noses of the local police. All you had to do was pay them off—them, and of course their bosses in city hall. Portland had a payoff system, going back well into the nineteenth century, which, as a general rule, worked so well no one bothered to notice it.

Then, one day in the spring of 1956, it all blew up in everyone's faces—with newspaper exposés, indictments of public officials, including the chief of police, the district attorney, and the mayor, and shameful national headlines. The town was in a tizzy.

Things got so far out of hand that in the spring of 1957, Bobby Kennedy, then a young lawyer for the Senate Rackets Committee, hauled two dozen or so of the town's most colorful characters back to Washington, D.C., where he grilled them before a national television audience.

TEMPEST STORM kept things lively at the Capitol.

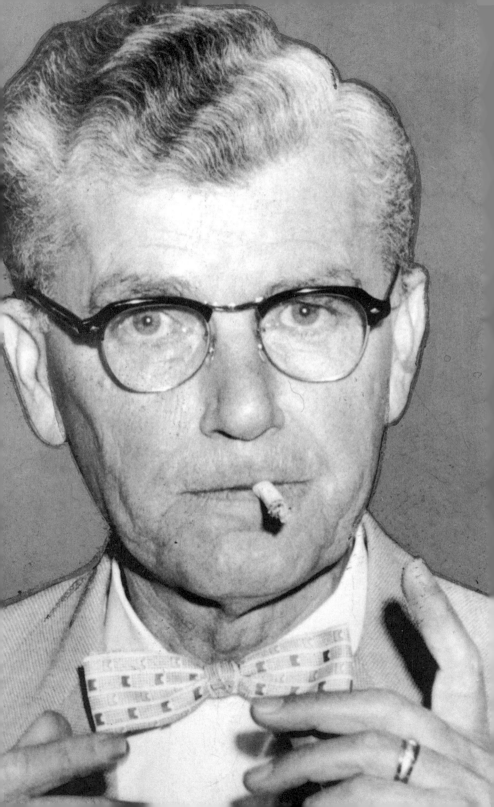

Never mind that his chief witness was the city's crime boss, a smooth-talking ex-con by the name of Jim Elkins—who, as a fairly careful reading of police reports as well as interviews with old madams and police officers reveals, probably never told the truth unless he had to. But it was undoubtedly good television.

A number of those invited to the Senate hearings, including the county's district attorney who had already been caught on tape planning to divvy up the payoff with some Seattle mobsters, simply invoked the Fifth Amendment. Portland's new mayor didn't take the Fifth, but he had his own problems with a lie detector test.

Finally, one of the Rackets Committee members had had enough. "It is embarrassing to me," he rumbled, "to think of the people of Portland, Oregon, with a mayor who flunks a lie-detector test and a district attorney hiding behind the Fifth Amendment. If I lived there, I would suggest they pull the flags down at half-mast in public shame."

> "I WOULD SUGGEST," SAID THE SENATOR, "THEY PULL THE FLAGS DOWN AT HALF-MAST IN PUBLIC SHAME."

Naturally, once the hearings were over, everyone came back home and did their best to forget that it ever happened. To be sure, there were indictments still to be dealt with, about 115 in all. But most of them wound up being dismissed for various technical reasons.

There was a handful of trials. But with one or two minor exceptions, none of the juries who heard them had the heart to find anyone guilty.

And so the great Portland vice scandal of the 1950s passed into a vast memory hole—one of those things polite people didn't talk about. For nearly a half century now, it has been Portland's biggest dirty little secret.

Not any more.

CRIME BOSS Jim Elkins ran the city.

NIPPY CONSTANTINO lies dead of gunshot wounds at the Sky Room on S.W. Park, Oct. 23, 1944. Note cigarette still burning in his left hand.

1

NO MONEY CHANGED HANDS

THE records show they let James Butler Elkins out of the Arizona State Penitentiary in July of 1937. Five years hard time under the desert sun, but it could have been a whole lot worse, considering.

As Elkins would explain some years later, the reason he got locked up this time was a warehouse robbery gone bad. Much to his

14

chagrin, gunfire had broken out—and Elkins, who of course wouldn't have fired unless fired upon, winged one of the cops. He was apprehended after a two-hour car chase. The judge called it assault with intent to kill and sentenced him to twenty to thirty years in the state prison. So, everything considered, five years might not have been such a bad deal at all.

Not surprisingly, the records don't show how much cash it took to buy Elkins his way out, either. But we can be pretty sure that it was his older brother Fred who came up with it, because Jim headed north from Arizona to Portland, Oregon, where he and Fred went into business together.

His kind of town.

IN THE LATE 1800s, the primary vice in Portland was selling sailors into servitude on sailing vessels. Sometimes the unfortunate seamen were plied with booze and kidnapped by "crimps." More often than not, they were sold by boardinghouse operators to pay off debts they'd run up. The shanghaiing, as it was called, got so out of hand that around the turn of the century, the British government threatened to declare the port of Portland off-limits to all British ships.

> OF 547 HOTELS, APARTMENTS, AND ROOMING HOUSES, INVESTIGATORS SAID, 431 WERE "WHOLLY GIVEN UP TO IMMORALITY."

After shanghaiing, prostitution became the vice of the moment. In 1911, a vice commission noted that of the 547 hotels, apartments, and rooming houses it inspected, 431 were "wholly given up to immorality." The problem was eventually resolved by an understanding that prostitution be confined to the North End, as the old-timers still call that part of the city north of Burnside and west of the Willamette River.

POLICE HEADQUARTERS at Southwest 2nd and Oak—or "Second and Hardwood," as the officers called it.

HARRY HUERTH, the "boxman," knocked off drugstores and gave the narcotics to Elkins.

During Prohibition, Portland was a major transshipment point for illegal whiskey from Canada. According to an old vice cop who wrote a book about those days, at any given time there were as many as one hundred speakeasies in the city, plus an equal number of beer and wine taverns. The police, who arrested rumrunners and bootleggers who failed to make the proper arrangements, kept so much confiscated booze in the basement of the police station at Second and Oak, they were able to effectively control the price of whiskey in the city by how much they put on the market.

And of course there was always gambling. Portland offered a full range of games of chance. Horse racing, dog racing, card rooms, dice. Slot machines—one-armed bandits—were all the rage.

PROHIBITION, OF COURSE, had ended by the time Elkins arrived in Portland. But thanks to a State Liquor Commission that kept the price of booze unnaturally high, the low-lying city of 300,000 on the banks of the Willamette still had an active trade in illegal alcohol, as well as all the other traditional vices.

An old-time safecracker, or "boxman," by the name of Harry Huerth remembers meeting Elkins shortly after his arrival.

"I was waiting on a corner and they drove up in a car," Huerth says. "I got in and was very much impressed with Jim's eyes at the time. I never will forget them. They were blue and just like ice. No feeling or anything there. I found out later he was that way, too. Jim at that time was a pimp. He owned a whorehouse and three or four girls were working in it. That's about all he had. But he was well on his way because he had a marvelous personality and everybody liked him. All the thieves would come down to visit him, the high-class professional thieves. Even at that early period he had a lot of connections with the police department."

> "I GOT IN AND WAS VERY MUCH IMPRESSED WITH JIM'S EYES ... THEY WERE BLUE AND JUST LIKE ICE. NO FEELING OR ANYTHING THERE."

Soon afterward, Huerth found himself knocking off drugstores for

Elkins. Elkins actually paid him a weekly salary to do it. Huerth's job was to find the store, rob it, then bring all the narcotics to Elkins, who—despite his later claims to the contrary—was a lifelong addict. Huerth was allowed to keep any money he found.

Next Elkins got Huerth a job working as a repairman for a fellow named Rayden Enloe, who at that time had a slot and pinball machine business. Enloe was a country boy who'd get drunk and light his cigars with hundred dollar bills.

Jim's brother Fred was also working for Enloe, and once or twice Huerth overheard Jim and Fred discussing how they were going to take over Enloe's business. He knew something was up, but he wasn't sure what.

"HE JUST TOLD THE GUYS FROM THEN ON THEY WERE WORKING FOR HIM. THAT'S THE WAY IT WAS. ENLOE WAS OUT. NO MONEY CHANGED HANDS OR ANYTHING."

"I'll never forget it," says Huerth. One day he was at work in Enloe's warehouse when Jim and Fred walked in. Jim was carrying a double-barreled shotgun. "Fred went in the office and told Enloe that they were taking over. One of the slot machine mechanics got scared and started to leave. Jim took the shotgun, reached out with it and stuck it between his legs and tripped him. He was very calm and collected with no excitement or nothing. He just told the guys from then on they were working for him. That's the way it was. Enloe was out. No money changed hands or anything."

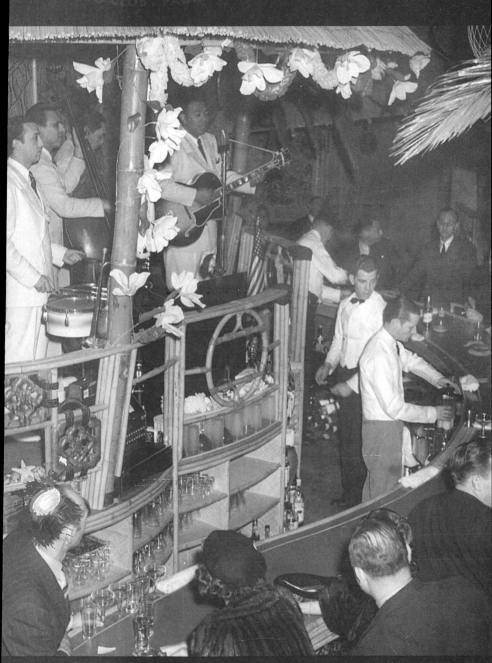

THE PAGO PAGO, owned by Al Winter, was the hot spot in town after the war.

A Tale of Two Rounders

BY THE LATE 1940s, Jim Elkins was a player, but still a minor one, in the city's booming vice economy. Top banana at the time was an intriguing fellow by the name of Al Winter. Winter owned the Pago Pago downtown at 525 Southwest Stark: bamboo furniture and Chinese cuisine.

On the second floor was a full-service gambling joint called the Turf Club, which operated so openly that the results of the latest races were sometimes announced from its windows to crowds waiting on the sidewalk below. The Turf Club was hooked up to the race wire, which, it should be noted, was controlled by the national crime syndicate. If you didn't know better, you might think Al was connected.

According to local legend, the storied mobster Bugsy Siegel stopped off in Portland during the war years to talk with Al. Naturally, all accounts are secondhand, because everyone directly involved is dead now, but it makes sense. As the story goes, they even considered establishing a Las Vegas–like casino complex on Sauvie Island—that flat expanse of agricultural and marshland, about forty miles square, located north of Portland where the Willamette and Columbia Rivers meet. The plan was abandoned after Siegel visited Portland one day, and it didn't stop raining the whole time he was here.

What *is* well documented is that, in the days before World War II, syndicate boss Meyer Lansky sent Siegel west to take over the race wire. Using their usual tools of persuasion, Bugsy and his thugs— among them, a young punk by the name of Mickey Cohen—quickly won the hearts and minds of bookies up and down the West Coast. It probably didn't hurt, either, when the owner of the competing wire service, James Ragan, was gunned down in Chicago. Never one to buck the tides of history, Al Winter went along.

STORIED MOBSTER Bugsy Siegel reportedly stopped off in Portland.

AL WINTER—If you didn't know better, you might think he was connected.

The son of a judge, and a lawyer himself, Winter ran the Portland rackets with a deft hand. A federal report from that time shows he controlled all the gambling in town. He hobnobbed with the city's rich and powerful. Federal judge Gus Solomon, whose name now graces the federal courthouse, and Oregon Supreme Court judge Lamar Tooze came to his Portland Heights home for dinner. Every Christmas he wrote large checks to the Catholic charities—but don't let that fool you.

Once, a couple of local hoods—rounders, as they called themselves then—decided to go to Seaside and knock over a few slot machines. One of them, a member of one of Portland's foremost criminal families by the name of Blackie Charlesworth, was a master at the game: while your partner was playing a machine, you'd sidle up next to it and drill a hole through the side. If you knew what you were doing, you hit the right wire, and the machine would start paying off like crazy. Then all you had to do was collect your money and beat it before anyone got wise.

> "THE PROBLEM IS, YOU DIDN'T GET MY PERMISSION. NOW I WANT FIFTY PERCENT OF EVERYTHING YOU GOT, AND IF YOU DO IT AGAIN, WE'LL BREAK YOUR HANDS."

The two rounders had been back in Portland a day or so when the phone rang in Charlesworth's apartment. Al Winter was on the other end of the line, very cool and collected. "Look," said Al, "I know what you did. The problem is, you didn't get my permission. Now I want fifty percent of everything you got, and if you do it again, we'll break your hands."

Al could be like that, too, when he had to.

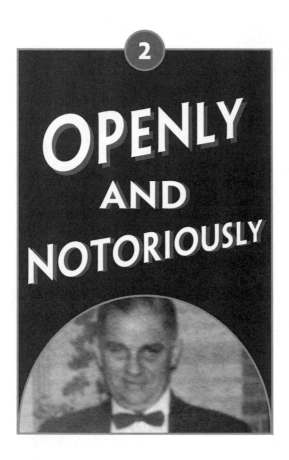

OPENLY AND NOTORIOUSLY

2

PERHAPS the best measure of Winter's success as a purveyor of forbidden pleasures was a 1948 City Club report, which noted that prostitution and gambling had been carried out "openly and notoriously throughout the city for a period of several years past." The report counted 248 different places within the city "where gambling, prostitution and other forms of vice were known to exist." On the west side alone, they found eleven houses of prostitution, five bookie joints, and eight

LITTLE RUSTY had a house, locat appropriately enough at Southw 1st and Hooker.

bootleggers with a "considerable assortment of safe burglars, stick-up men, dope peddlers and other underworld characters" doing business in the city.

"Most of the gambling," the report continued, "is carried on openly and is available to any customer willing to hazard a few dollars. Banks of gaudy slot machines or dice tables are usually busy accessories adjacent to the bar. Chinese gambling establishments operate more furtively and behind a door with the usual peep-hole. Poker is played in most of the card rooms, the house dealing and banking the game."

> THE CITY HAD BECOME A REFUGE FOR UNDERWORLD TYPES, LIVING IN PORTLAND WITH "THE KNOWLEDGE AND TACIT CONSENT OF THE POLICE."

Not only that, continued the report, but the city had become a "refuge" for underworld types, living in Portland with "the knowledge and tacit consent of the police." Portland, in fact, was a base of operations for a gang of safecrackers that operated throughout the western states. They were allowed to live in the city as long as they refrained from knocking off local businesses, and made their payments to the appropriate authorities.

The rackets in the city itself, the report said, were controlled by "syndicates." They took their cut by "leasing" equipment and locations to the operators. The going rate for protection from police was $50 per slot machine, $500 a month for dice tables, and $1,000 a month or more for poker. The report estimated that the total payoff to the police was about $60,000 a month. That would be about half a million in present-day dollars.

IT WAS AN ENVIRONMENT in which Elkins could be expected to grow and prosper, although life was not without its ups and downs. Shortly after his arrival in Portland, he was caught picking up a package of heroin at the train station and sentenced to a year in Leavenworth. Whether the heroin was for his own use or for business purposes is unknown.

The coin machine business—slots and pinball—could also get dicey on occasion, as Elkins jockeyed with competitors for a piece of the local market. On one occasion, when Elkins and one of his employees "repossessed" a couple of slot machines in Beaverton, the repossessee started shooting, putting a couple of bullet holes in Elkins's car and one in his side. Elkins was arrested, but later acquitted when the key witnesses against him failed to show up at trial.

Otherwise business was good. In addition to his coin machine business, Elkins acquired a few after-hours drinking and gambling joints. His coin machine business, called the Service Machine Co., had an office and warehouse at 1426 Second Avenue, where KOIN Tower is now located. According to Huerth, who became a one-third partner in the business, they kept four or five goons in the office at all times. Whenever there was any trouble at the clubs—usually a longshoreman taking out his frustrations on a slot machine with a grappling hook, or a thieving bartender—they sent down the goon squad to give the offender a beating, or dumping, as it was then called.

> WHENEVER THERE WAS ANY TROUBLE AT THE CLUBS, THEY SENT DOWN THE GOON SQUAD TO GIVE THE OFFENDER A BEATING, OR DUMPING, AS IT WAS THEN CALLED.

ELKINS WAS MOVING UP. He no longer depended on Huerth to steal his narcotics for him. As Huerth reports, Elkins had found a doctor in Sellwood to supply him. That would be Dr. Donald Nickelsen, a larger-than-life character who ministered to the local underworld and frequently made the Portland papers with his big-game hunting expeditions to Africa. On one of them, in 1948, Nickelsen reportedly bagged a record gazelle, two types of zebra, two lions, an elephant, a warthog, and two species of antelope.

On another, "he came off second-best in an encounter with a charging 2000-pound Rhodesian buffalo" that "snapped his shoulder like matchwood and left horn punctures in his upper arm." The good doctor rode around town with a full-grown cheetah in the backseat of his convertible.

Police Find Body
Of Ship's Captain

3 JAILED, QUERIED ON DEATH

Additional Picture on Page 16

A week-old murder was uncovered early Tuesday when police found the battered body of Capt. Frank B. Tatum, 53, skipper of the S. S. Edwin Abbey of the Shepard Steamship company at the base of an embankment off N. W. Santa Anit terrace, Kings Heights, where it had been tossed some time Tuesday night, January 14.

Arrested in the Cecil club, 221 S. W. 6th avenue, on suspicion of murder, are Patrick O'Day, 40, of 761 S. W. Vista avenue, operator of the Cecil club; Harold E. Sehorn, 25, of 7648 N. E. Glisan street, and Johnny Snyder, 20, of 221 S. W. 6th avenue, known to the boxing ring as "Bobby Carter".

Search for Captain Tatum started late Monday with a routine investigation of a missing report by Earl Sanders and R. J. Evans, U. S. maritime commission, stating Tatum had been missing since January 14 and was believed to have had between $500 and $600 of his own money and about $150 of ship's funds.

Officers learned R. J. Peterson, steward of the Edwin Abbey had last seen Captain Tatum in front of 221 S. W. 6th avenue in mid-afternoon of January 14.

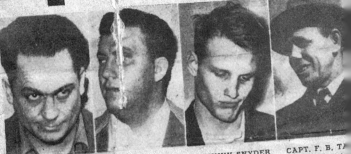

PATRICK O'DAY   HAROLD E. SEHORN   JOHNNY SNYDER   CAPT. F. B. T.

Patrick O'Day, Harold E. Sehorn and Johnny Snyder were arrested Tuesday on suspicion of the murder of Captain Frank B. Tatum, believed to have been beaten in O'Day's night 221 S. W. 6th avenue, and rolled, still moaning, hours later, down a Kings Heights

Police learned Captain Tatum had been drinking in the Cecil club earlier in the day. Sehorn and Snyder, found at the club, admitted, police said, hauling the body from the club in O'Day's automobile about 9 P. M. January 14 to the west side hills and dropping it over an embankment.

Sehorn and Snyder took the officers to the scene at 3 A. M. Tuesday and the body was found where it had rolled some 50 feet down an embankment off N. W. Santa Anita terrace toward Barnes road.

The body was removed to the coroner's office, where an autopsy was to be performed.

Snyder and Sehorn, Police Capt. James Purcell said, told him of an altercation in the club about 7 P. M. January 14 between Tatum and O'Day and said O'Day beat Tatum, leaving him for several hours moaning

in a room. Shortly before 9 P. M. O'Day told them "to get him out of here," the men related.

They said they carried Tatum from the club to the automobile, drove to the west side and "while the man was still slightly moaning," tossed him down the bank.

O'Day refused to answer questions of police and denied implication. However, he offered the explanation that a couple of days before, Tatum had borrowed $100 from him and they had an argument about 2:30 P. M. Tuesday regarding the money. He denied injuring Tatum and said Tatum left the club of his own volition.

Later in the day, officers took Frank Davis, 129 S. E. 80th avenue, into custody and booked him as a material witness after Snyder was said to have given him a package containing an $1800 platinum watch and a cameo ring belong-

ing to Tatum. Davis a Snyder gave him a p police stated, but said he knowledge of its conte that O'Day received it when he appeared at home and requested it. said he was told by C give the package to D

Shortly after the Tatum was found Capt cell and squad raided club and arrested bet and 30 persons for bein barred doors, most b leased under $100 b questioning.

Two, though, Leo Stanley, 40, U. S. na Clifford R. Marson, 24 N. E. Brazee street, v for further investigati Tatum's widow, Vir said to reside at 19 M nue N., Billerica, Mas of the St. Andrews h she visited Captain Ta while he was in port 2 to 18.

Part of Huerth's job, now that he was no longer needed to steal drugs for Elkins, was to ride around every night with a guy called Jack the Pencil—so called because he was good at math—and collect Elkins's share of the take from the joints he owned or bankrolled. "Jack would figure up the percentages of the whiskey used and collect from the club manager who was always some kind of a thief who would try to beat him if he could. But Jack was a pretty smart kid. By the time we got through we would have quite a large amount of money to take back to the office."

They Just Wanted His Watch

CAPTAIN FRANK TATUM of the S.S. *Edwin Abbey* had been drinking his fool head off for several days, flashing a large wad of bills all over town. Naturally, this caught the attention of certain parties who make it their business to know about such things. That and the diamond-studded platinum wristwatch he showed off in just about every club he hit.

The good captain was last seen by the ship's steward, standing outside the Cecil Club at 221 Southwest Sixth Avenue on the night of January 14, 1947. When his disappearance was reported several days later, the police started turning up the heat on the Portland underworld. It was one thing for gambling and prostitution to operate openly in the city, but murder was something else again. And if the police had to close down all the illegal establishments in town until someone came forward with a little information, that's how it was going to be.

THE NEWSPAPER STORIES say the case was solved when detectives discovered a man who worked at the Cecil sporting the diamond-studded platinum watch. An old vice cop, who was around at the time, says that's not exactly how it happened. The tip that led to the arrests actually came from Jim Elkins himself. Elkins would certainly have been in a position to know about the Tatum murder, since it was his men who did it.

To be perfectly fair, they hadn't planned to kill anyone.

CAPTAIN TATUM'S MURDER was just one thing too many.

O'Day Denies He Kicked Captain; Disputes Testimony of Witnesses

BY PAUL F. EWING
Staff Writer, The Oregonian

Patrick O'Day, on trial for first degree murder before Circuit Judge James R. Bain, took the witness stand Friday to deny kicking or jumping on Capt. Frank B. Tatum during progress of a fight in O'Day's Cecil rooms "night club," 221 S. W. 6th avenue, last January 14.

The state contends the 53-year-old master of the steamship Edwin Abbey was beaten and kicked to death in that fight, before his body was dumped on N. W. Santanita terrace, near Hermosa boulevard.

"I definitely did not kick the captain at any time," O'Day said, also denying that he jumped on the captain. "I never jump on anyone, particularly someone I liked as I did the captain."

Tatum was snoring—"good old healthy snores"—after he fell by a radiator, O'Day testified. The captain did not rise again.

O'Day denied telling John Snyder, 20, who pleaded guilty to a reduced charge of manslaughter and turned state's evidence, to go through Tatum's pockets, although he said he saw Snyder doing so. He also denied telling Snyder and Harold E. Sehorn, 25, of 7648 N. E. Glisan street, who also pleaded guilty to manslaughter and testified for the state, to dump Tatum in the park or up the hill.

He did not know Tatum was dead until Snyder told him on January 17, O'Day declared.

On direct examination by Defense Attorney John Patrick Hannon, O'Day asserted he last saw Tatum's $450 platinum and diamond wrist watch and Tatum's ring when he saw John Snyder wearing them

caused the fight—that he gave Tatum when the latter failed to finish his second five jiggers of whisky.

He said Tatum hit him, that he apologized, but Tatum persisted and hit him again. He struck a blow across the bar which knocked Tatum down, he said, but he still tried to stop Tatum from fighting.

Blows were interspersed with periods of argument. Finally O'Day said, Tatum "looked like he was going to hit me again so I hit him," Tatum fell against the end of the bar, rose, "sort of walked around in a circle and fell. I don't know if he hit the radiator."

Tatum als

Patrick Gene O'Day, 37 (right), took the witness stand in his own defense Friday as his first degree murder trial neared its end. Circuit Judge James R. Bain (left) approached its end.

been purchased at least six or seven years before for use on hunting and fishing trips.

Previous testimony by other witnesses that she never had seen O'Day wear glasses until he appeared in the courtroom with them was explained by O'Day. He said he had owned glasses since 1943, that he had very good eyes but they tired easily and he wore the glasses to rest them.

Name Changed Legally

Cross-examination disclosed that O'Day legally became Patrick Gene O'Day in 1945 or early in 1946, because he had been known under that name

All they wanted was the sea captain's money—and, of course, his watch. The papers said it was worth $1,800, which would be about ten times that much in today's dollars. In any case, as "Diamond Jim" Purcell, chief of detectives at the time, understood, it certainly wasn't Elkins's fault.

As the record makes clear, Elkins was a longtime snitch. That's how you play the vice game: turn in your competition, and in exchange, the cops cut you a free pass. And if sometimes you have to rat on your own people, too—in this case, Patrick O'Day, the forty-year-old ex-boxer who managed the Cecil—well, that's life.

In any case, O'Day took the fall and went off to prison, the police took the heat off Elkins—and by all rights, it should have been back to business as usual in Portland. But it didn't work out quite that way.

The lurid murder of a sea captain in a downtown club was apparently just one thing too many for the good people of Portland to abide. The Portland City Club, which prided itself as a bastion of progressive ideas, convened a special committee to investigate Portland's deplorable crime problem.

DURING THE WAR YEARS, a single syndicate had controlled all gambling operations within the city. Since the end of the war, it had split into two groups that handled different aspects of the gambling business. Perhaps out of politeness, the report didn't mention either Winter or Elkins by name, but everybody had to know who they were talking about. In addition, the report said, "another large operator from Clackamas County has apparently established himself in Portland." That would be a flamboyant character named Lonnie Logsdon, who rode his palomino in the Rose Festival parade each June.

The City Club report couldn't have said anything the people of Portland didn't already know—since, as the report itself stated, the city's vice industry operated quite openly. Nevertheless, reform fever was in the air.

JOEY CLEMO, the "Shoeshine Boy," later became one of Elkins's toughs.

"No Sin" Lee to the Rescue

IN JANUARY 1949, Dorothy McCullough Lee, a prim, well-bred woman who had previously served in the state legislature, became Portland's first woman mayor, replacing Earl Riley—who, as the historian E. Kimbark MacColl has noted, ranks right up there among the most corrupt mayors in Portland's history. He even had a special safe installed in the mayor's office to keep his share of the payoff.

Dorothy Lee, on the other hand, was so clean she almost squeaked. Upon taking office, she appointed an elderly former head of the State Police by the name of Charles Pray as her new police chief, and together they launched a war on vice.

DOROTHY MCCULLOUGH LEE, A PRIM, WELL-BRED WOMAN WHO HAD PREVIOUSLY SERVED IN THE STATE LEGISLATURE WAS SO CLEAN SHE ALMOST SQUEAKED.

First, they went after the slots. Slot machines, the equivalent of today's video poker, had been against the law in Portland for years, but everybody played them. Country clubs like the Waverly and the Columbia Edgewater had slot machines. For that matter, so did the Press Club.

The same federal report that shows Al Winter controlling the gambling joints in Portland says a guy named Lester Beckman owned the slot machines in all of them. Slot machines—one-armed bandits— were money machines, pure and simple. As the mob well knew, they were also quite useful for laundering profits from other illegal enterprises.

There's a story, told by one of Lester Beckman's sons, about how Lester once took a trip to Chicago, where the slot machines were manufactured, and returned with a model that took silver dollars. Apparently, it was the first silver dollar machine in Portland. As soon as he hit town, Beckman dropped it off at the Pago Pago and went

LONNIE LOGSDON ran the rackets in Clackamas County.

home to rest up. About an hour later, he got a call from the manager of the club to come down and take care of his damn machine. It wouldn't work any more. "What's the matter?" asked Beckman, considerably annoyed. "Did it break down?" "No," said the manager, "it's full!"

LESTER BECKMAN,
slot machine king.

After taking on the slots, the mayor and her handpicked chief of police raided some Chinese gambling joints, which ran the Chinese lottery. After that, they turned their attention to the downtown card rooms, where they attempted to enforce the betting limits on poker.

Next, "No Sin" Lee, as she came to be known, got the city council to pass a law outlawing pinball machines. Although it was certainly possible for players to redeem games won for dimes and quarters, no one really believed that pinball machines were gambling devices on the order of slot machines. They were, however, to use a current phrase, considered a sort of "gateway" device that might lead unwary teenagers to slot machines.

The new pinball law was promptly challenged in court, and it would be another five years before the U.S. Supreme Court itself declared Portland's law against pinball machines constitutional. In the meantime, the subject of pinball machines would dominate the political discourse of the city. That and, of course, striptease dancing, which was also considered dangerous to the public morality.

Not too surprisingly, none of this got to the heart of the city's deeply embedded vice culture. Under Dorothy Lee, the payoff continued—but now it simply went around the mayor and the chief of police. Earl Riley, the former mayor, managed it from his Packard dealership on Burnside.

"NO SIN" LEE set out to clean up the town.

As one former madam recalls, the brothels north of Burnside on Second and Third Avenues continued to operate as if nothing had happened. Other gambling and prostitution operations simply moved outside the city limits, into the wilds of Multnomah County, or Clackamas County to the south—most notoriously, the Fireside in Milwaukie, which was owned by Lonnie Logsdon.

It was all enough, however, to convince Al Winter that there were better ways of making a living. In 1950 Winter moved his base of operations to Las Vegas, where, with the help of a good deal of money from the Los Angeles mob, he and several others started the Sahara, the first big casino-hotel on the Strip. In 1951, the Pago Pago and the Turf Club closed for good.

It could have been a lot worse. In 1951, Lester Beckman, who obviously didn't have the same sort of connections that Winter had, was convicted of income tax evasion and sentenced to two years in McNeil Island, the federal penitentiary in Puget Sound by Seattle.

"In Memory of a Smile"

DESPITE THE BEST intentions of Dorothy McCullough Lee, prostitution was indeed continuing unabated in the North End. We have this from no less an authority than a woman known as Little Rusty, who had arrived in Portland just as the new mayor was taking office. Five-feet-one-inch tall, and pretty in a sweet and sultry way that men seemed to like.

> LITTLE RUSTY, FIVE-FEET-ONE-INCH TALL ,WAS PRETTY IN A SWEET AND SULTRY WAY THAT MEN SEEMED TO LIKE.

Little Rusty, by this time in her late twenties, was a coal miner's daughter from Harlan County, Kentucky. While still a teenager, she had set out on her own, settling for a while in Detroit, where, during the World War II years, she got her start as a dime-a-dance girl. The rest just came naturally—"instinct," as she puts it.

Before long, she'd hooked up with a shakedown artist who used

LITTLE RUSTY knew something about the legal profession, too.

JUSTICE WILLIAM O. DOUGLAS came to Portland to have a good time, frequently with Little Rusty.

the alias Billy Cavenaugh, who took her to Chicago and then Los Angeles. After a short stay in San Francisco, it was on to the great Pacific Northwest.

In Portland, she drew the attention of U.S. Supreme Court Justice William O. Douglas, who used to frequent the wide-open city on the banks of the Willamette. At the time, Douglas—remembered now primarily as a great champion of civil liberties, as well as the author of numerous books about his adventures as an outdoorsman and world traveler—was a significant player on the national political scene. His patron, Joseph Kennedy, had seen to it that Douglas succeeded him as head of the Securities and Exchange Commission when he left that post to become Franklin D. Roosevelt's ambassador to Great Britain.

Douglas had narrowly missed becoming Roosevelt's running mate in 1944 when, at the nominating convention, party leaders supporting Harry Truman switched the order of names on a list of candidates given them by Roosevelt. In other words, if fate had dealt the cards a bit differently, Douglas would have been president of the United States by this time. Instead, when he could find the time, the brilliant jurist was hanging out in Portland, often in the company of Little Rusty.

Rusty remembers sitting in the Clover Room, then one of the town's hottest nightclubs, with Douglas and his friend, local industrialist Damon Trout, watching Sammy Davis Jr. perform with his father and uncle as the Will Mastin Trio. It's not generally known that Sammy got his start in Portland, playing at a variety of spots around town for two years before, out of the blue, Frank Sinatra sent a telegram summoning the act to New York to open for him at the Capitol Theater.

In his autobiography, Sammy says they couldn't believe their good fortune. They passed that telegram around like three drunks working on the same bottle. But while they were still here, posters with Sammy's picture were all over town.

Douglas's friend Damon Trout, who owned a plant that manufactured electronic gear for ships, can best be described as an intermediary between Portland society and the town's underworld. If someone needed to set up visiting dignitaries with female company for an evening, Trout would be

SAMMY DAVIS JR. at the Clover Club.

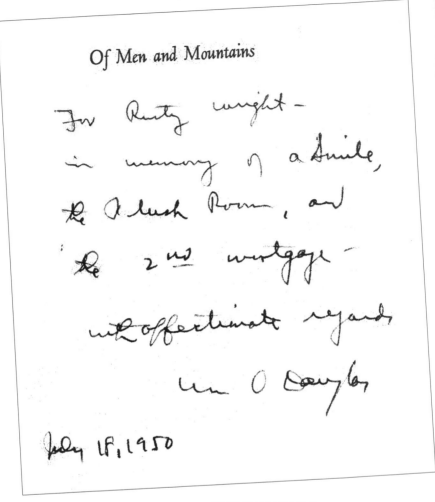

For Rusty tonight —
in memory of a Smile,
& a lush Room, and
& 2nd mortgage —

with affectionate regards

Wm O Douglas

July 18, 1950

JUSTICE DOUGLAS'S inscription to Rusty.

the one to call. For example, it was he who introduced the justice to Little Rusty.

At his manufacturing plant on Northwest Vaughn, he also maintained a private nightclub called the Plush Room where public officials of sufficient status mingled with elements of the Portland underworld. High-ranking police officers were given keys to the Plush Room, so that they could help themselves to its well-stocked bar at any time of day or night.

Little Rusty and the visiting Supreme Court justice also spent many hours together at the Plush Room. In fact, in the summer of 1950, Douglas gave her a copy of his new book, *Of Men and Mountains,* with the inscription: "For Rusty Wright—in memory of a Smile, the Plush Room, and the 2nd mortgage." A "smile," Rusty remembers, was a drink. She can't remember what a "second mortgage" was supposed to be.

Rusty also recalls hanging out of a third-story window of the Benson Hotel with Douglas, waving and shouting at Clackamas County rackets boss Lonnie Logsdon as he rode past on his palomino in the Rose Festival parade.

If only they'd known: On March 31, 1951, the front page of the *Oregonian* carried the news of a massive crackdown on gambling in Clackamas County. More than one hundred night spots, including the Fireside, owned by Logsdon, had been raided by the State Police. According to the old vice cop, a good bit of the information used by the state troopers came from—you'll never guess—Jim Elkins.

With Al Winter in Las Vegas, and Lonnie Logsdon now effectively out of business, Elkins had to be grinning.

MARCH 31, 1951 Logsdon was finished.

STAR-GAZING at the Star Theater

THE old vice cop, the one who saw it all, remembers the first time he became aware of the payoff. He was a rookie then, working as a beat cop in the North End. One day his partner, an old-timer on the force, called in sick and asked him to come by the house before work. When the rookie got there, he was handed a list with several names and addresses on it. "Just tell 'em Ron sent you," said the older cop. The rookie did as he was told, and at each stop he was handed a sealed envelope, which he then dutifully delivered to his partner. By this time, of course, he'd figured out what was up. But if there's one thing he'd already learned, it was this: Keep your eyes open and your mouth shut. And for the next fifty years—until just recently, as a matter of fact—that's what he did.

> KEEP YOUR EYES OPEN AND YOUR MOUTH SHUT, THE OLD COP SAID. AND FOR THE NEXT FIFTY YEARS, THAT'S WHAT HE DID.

At the time, there were two payoffs operating within the Portland Police Bureau. The one the rookie officer had stumbled onto, easily the less significant of the two, involved individual beat officers making their own collections of perhaps ten or twenty dollars a month—"smile money," as it was called—from vice operators. The other payoff, which added up to hundreds of thousands of dollars a year, was the real grease that kept the city's vice economy moving. It was collected under the auspices of the captain of each precinct and then divvied up among higher-ranking police officers and the politicians at city hall.

There was actually a theory behind all this: Since there was going to be a certain amount of vice in the city anyway, it was reasoned, why not manage it and keep it under control? Say what you will, but there are those who will tell you that as a system of government, it worked as smoothly as what we have today. In any case, it was so much a part of the fabric of the society that most ordinary citizens probably didn't bother to notice it, unless it was brought to their attention, which it was, from time to time.

Not every Portland cop participated in the payoff system—but it's clear the bureau was run by those who did. Officers who refused, or just didn't catch on, were usually assigned to some job away from the action, such as the records division or the Southwest Precinct. According to their abilities and ambitions, others rose through the ranks. And during the early 1950s, none would rise farther or faster than an officer by the name of Jim Purcell—Diamond Jim, as he was called.

Diamond Jim Takes Charge

DIAMOND JIM WAS, by all accounts, an intelligent, charming, and capable man. According to a high-ranking officer who worked closely with Purcell for years, he was also "utterly dishonest." From the beginning of his career, the officer said, Purcell had only two thoughts in mind: one, to become chief; and two, "to make as much money as possible, regardless of means."

As a young officer, Purcell made a name for himself by recovering an unusually large number of stolen autos. Only later did someone figure out the secret to his success. An ex-con acquaintance of his would steal the cars, then drop them off at a prearranged spot where Purcell would happen upon them. Purcell's closest friend was a pimp and accused grave robber by the name of George Bernard, with whom he owned the Penguin Club just off Sandy Boulevard.

> PURCELL HAD ONLY TWO THOUGHTS IN MIND: ONE, TO BECOME CHIEF; AND TWO, "TO MAKE AS MUCH MONEY AS POSSIBLE, REGARDLESS OF MEANS."

To be perfectly honest, the only reason anyone knew Purcell owned a piece of the club in the first place is that Purcell got a little greedy. Acting in his capacity as a high-ranking police officer, he had reduced the Penguin's monthly payoff. Since this didn't make any sense, some of the other cops did a little investigating of their own. Presumably, Purcell was persuaded to restore the Penguin's payoff to its proper level.

During much of Dorothy McCullough Lee's term as mayor, Diamond Jim served as chief of detectives. No wonder her handpicked chief of police, Charles Pray, resigned in frustration, complaining at his final press conference that the police had kept him in the dark. "They don't even tell me where the gambling is taking place," he said.

And if the chief of police didn't know anything, you can imagine what Dorothy Lee knew. Jim Elkins, who, besides everything else, seemed to have a puckish sense of humor, opened a whorehouse in a hotel across the street from city hall, in full view of the mayor's office. The idea, after it had been up and running for a decent amount of time, was to have it raided by his friends on the vice squad, thereby causing the mayor no end of embarrassment in the press.

> **JIM ELKINS OPENED A WHOREHOUSE IN A HOTEL ACROSS THE STREET FROM CITY HALL, IN FULL VIEW OF THE MAYOR'S OFFICE.**

Unfortunately for Elkins, the old vice cop who was at that time the mayor's driver, and liked her personally, got wind of the plot and made sure the unauthorized operation was quietly dismantled. Dorothy, who was never told the true story, always thought the police had done a bang-up job.

Poor Dorothy Lee. Everybody was making fun of her. Especially the *Oregon Journal,* which ran poems on its front page that mocked her efforts to stamp out slot machines, pinball, and punchboards, which were something like today's scratch cards.

And then there was the matter of her hats. Like any other proper lady of that long-ago time, Dorothy Lee always wore a hat. And the gentlemen of the press—for there were hardly any women reporters then—made merry over those, too.

IN THE ELECTION OF 1952, the vice operators and the downtown business community—which was feeling the effects of the anti-vice campaign in terms of declining property values—got behind a candidate more to their liking than the scrupulous Dorothy Lee. His name was Fred Peterson. Peterson, a good old boy who ran a drugstore over by Grant High School, had served on the city council for the past decade.

The rumor on the streets was that once Peterson was elected, Elkins paid him $100,000 to appoint Diamond Jim Purcell as chief of police. Of course, we'll never know for sure if that was the exact amount. But whatever it was, it was worth it.

DIAMOND JIM PURCELL, the new police chief.

Back to Business As Usual

IT WAS BUSINESS AS USUAL again in the Rose City. As it had been for decades, the well-oiled rackets machine was now free to operate, more or less openly, under the protection of the city government.

At the head of the new administration was Fred Peterson. If he didn't understand the payoff system, no one did. Operating directly under Peterson was the new chief of police, Diamond Jim Purcell. Now that he was chief, he was even shaking down the gypsies, who at that time lived somewhat illegally in storefronts off West Burnside. For a mere $500 a month, Diamond Jim agreed to look the other way. And directly under Purcell, as head of the vice squad, was a wiry, intense man with a pencil-thin mustache by the name of Carl Crisp.

According to an officer who worked for him, Crisp was an extremely capable police officer and a meticulous reader of reports. If you didn't write something up in exactly the prescribed manner, he'd hand it back to you until you got it right—even if it meant that you had to stay up all night. The old vice cop says he learned a lot about police work from Crisp.

Unfortunately for all concerned, however, Crisp was also quite venal, and never missed an opportunity to use his position to weasel a few extra bucks out of anyone who depended on the good offices of the police. Perhaps it was due to his hardscrabble upbringing in Eastern Oregon, where his German-immigrant mother worked as a ranch cook—although there were certainly others, in those post-Depression times, who had experienced greater poverty. Or perhaps it had something to do with his reputed drug habit. If so, that would explain a lot. Elkins made a practice of getting those he worked with hooked on drugs. Hospital reports show that Crisp favored barbiturates in combination with alcohol.

Crisp kept a record of his multifarious illegal transactions in notebooks, with entries written in a German-based code. Whatever

HIS HONOR, PORTLAND'S NEW MAYOR, Fred Peterson.

else you might wish to say about him, Crisp was undoubtedly the right man for the job.

Archie Erskin, a bookie and gambler, found himself sitting in a patrol car with Crisp one night shortly after the Jo Ann Dewey murder, which everyone assumed was drug related. Erskin, who was opposed to drugs, asked Crisp why he didn't clean up the narcotics business in Portland.

> ERSKIN ASKED CRISP WHY HE DIDN'T CLEAN UP THE NARCOTICS BUSINESS IN PORTLAND. "WHY CUT OFF THE HAND THAT FEEDS YOU?" CRISP SAID.

"Why cut off the hand that feeds you?" asked Crisp. After that, says Erskin, he didn't trust the man. His instincts were good. Erskin would later be arrested when he refused to open up a gaming room downtown under Crisp's direct control.

Little Rusty remembers the time the vice squad lieutenant summoned her to his office at Second and Oak to ask for information on a well-known Portland pimp. By this time, Rusty had a house in the Corbett neighborhood—at Southwest First and Hooker, as a matter of fact—which became a sort of clubhouse over the years for a dozen or more Portland police officers. Every night, they'd pass the time playing cards in her kitchen.

Naturally, Rusty didn't tell Crisp anything. There's nothing she hates as much as a stool pigeon.

"If you're so smart, you should be able to find out yourself," she told him.

A short time later, they were dating. Crisp, who must have been between marriages at the time, wanted to marry her. He even gave her a ring. Nothing ever came of it, because her Police Bureau friends warned her off. They didn't trust him either. But in case you were wondering, she did keep the ring.

◄ *GYPSIES* lighting funeral candles.
► *CARL CRISP,* head of the vice squad.

Even Square Johns Can See

THINK OF IT, if you will, as an economic system, starting with the customers—who, for services rendered, give their money to vice operators—who, because the services they provide are illegal, need protection from the cops. But it's a two-way deal: in addition to making the monthly payoff, the racketeers are responsible for providing the cops with information on interlopers who may threaten their turf—a task, needless to say, they are only too happy to perform.

> **BUT EVEN THEY HAD TO WONDER JUST WHAT IN THE WORLD WAS GOING ON. AFTER ALL, IF THEY COULD SEE IT SO EASILY, WHY COULDN'T THE POLICE?**

And then there are all the associated jobs and industries—from the taxi drivers, to the clubs and restaurants, to the property owners and financiers—whose livelihoods depended on a thriving vice economy.

In fact, when it was working properly, there was something in it for just about everyone. Everyone, that is, except the square johns, as they were called at the time, who had no interest in the profits or pleasures of the vice economy.

But even *they* had to wonder from time to time—since the vice operations were once again being carried out openly—just what in the world was going on. After all, if they could see it so easily, why couldn't the police? This was a problem.

And so, to keep up appearances, the police occasionally had to raid some of the "authorized" establishments, as well as those that weren't.

The entrance to the Market Club still exists at 925 Southeast Tenth, in the middle of what was once the old Italian produce row. In the front of the Market Club was a counter that served breakfast and lunch to the hundreds of truck farmers and buyers who would come each day to parcel out the city's rations. In the back was a bustling little gambling den, with slot machines, two pool tables, a ticker-tape for the race wire, and three or four tables where farmers who stopped by for a bit of relaxation after selling their loads would invariably get fleeced.

"They didn't have a chance," recalls Joe Gatto, whose father owned the building and operated an adjoining produce business, Gatto & Sons—"not playing against the two or three house gamblers that were sitting at their table. There'd be a fight in there every day." Some of the more seasoned card players, Joe recalls, played with loaded revolvers on the table.

Joe also remembers how, the night before a raid, they'd always get a call from the chief, Diamond Jim Purcell himself. Then they'd move all their gambling paraphernalia into the cooler. And when the police arrived—or more to the point, the press, which was always invited to ride along to witness the great event—there was nothing to see except a couple of old Italian truck farmers shooting pool.

> JOE REMEMBERS HOW, THE NIGHT BEFORE A RAID, THEY'D ALWAYS GET A CALL FROM THE CHIEF, DIAMOND JIM PURCELL HIMSELF.

It was not that the members of the press were so much denser than the general population that they didn't also suspect something more was going on. But as they all quickly learned, there were rewards—if only a chance to ride along with the police and scoop the opposition—for not looking too closely at what was really going on.

Some inducements were even more tangible. The *Oregonian's* police reporter received a monthly retainer of $50 from certain Chinese gambling houses to ensure that, in the event of a raid, he would report the names of clients incorrectly. The sum would be left on the counter for him each month.

And every year around Christmas time, Elkins and the other major racketeer in town, Stan Terry, who controlled the payoff in outlying Multnomah County, would send a case of whiskey to the boys in the newsrooms of the *Journal* and *Oregonian*.

It seems that just about everybody had a role to play in the vice economy.

"John's Other Wife"

UNDER DOROTHY "NO SIN" LEE, Portland had become a desert, not just for pinball and punchboards, but for striptease dancing as well. That changed when good old boy Fred Peterson ascended to the mayor's office in January 1953. Not just one, but two downtown burlesque houses—the Star, just north of the corner of Northwest Sixth and Burnside, and the Capitol, at Fourth and Morrison—opened to a land-office business.

For one shining moment in Portland history—before a scandal that made the pages of *Life Magazine* caused her to leave town—the famous stripper Tempest Storm performed regularly at the Capitol. The Tantalizing Miss Candy Renee, a dark-haired, willowy woman, whose real name according to police documents was Betty Roth, held forth at the Star. With Candy and Tempest in town, there was always plenty of competition for the burlesque dollar.

> **TEMPEST STORM PERFORMED AT THE CAPITOL. CANDY RENEE HELD FORTH AT THE STAR. IT WAS A BATTLE OF THE G-STRINGS.**

It was, as the *Oregon Journal* so delicately phrased it, a "Battle of the G-strings." And it all started, as Tempest herself recalls in her autobiography, down in Los Angeles, where she'd been dancing at the Follies. At that particular time, she had just broken off an affair with Sammy Davis Jr.—who it should be noted for posterity, was one of a dozen or so former lovers including Mickey Rooney, Elvis, Engelbert Humperdinck, John Kennedy, and last but not least, Vic Damone, chronicled and examined in her memoir.

"As my passion for Sammy Davis Jr. cooled," she said, "I turned my affections toward John Becker, a former singer and burlesque straight man," who, it developed, "was very good as both a lover and a manager." Unfortunately, however, John had an ex-wife, also a stripper, by the name of Arabella Andre, who wouldn't leave the happy couple alone.

To hear Arabella's version of it, Becker had married Tempest before their divorce was final—thereby, in her mind at least, making her Becker's legal wife. She was a bit obsessive on the subject. Once, to make her point, she had put sugar in the gas tank of Tempest's new pink Cadillac. On several occasions, Arabella threatened to throw acid in Tempest's face, thereby scarring her for life.

So to get away from her, Tempest and John moved to Portland in the fall of 1953, where they purchased the Capitol Theater, and went into business for themselves.

But if Tempest thought that they would find happiness and contentment on the banks of the Willamette, Candy Renee, who not only performed but managed the Star as well, had other ideas. Which is surely not to suggest that Candy was acting on anything more sinister than good promotional instincts when she hired Arabella Andre as a headliner at the Star—and billed her on the marquee as "John's Other Wife."

ONE NIGHT THE DOORBELL rang at Tempest and Johnny's Portland apartment, and Tempest opened the door to find Arabella standing there with a highball glass in her hand. Arabella threw the contents of the glass at Tempest. Tempest screamed, thinking that her stage career was over.

As it turned out, there was only water in the glass. But enough was enough. The Beckers called the police and had Arabella committed to a mental institution. After five days, Arabella, having been declared sane, was released. She sued the Beckers for false arrest, asking $35,000 in damages. A month later, the whole sordid tale— "Burlesque Wives War in Portland"—turned up in *Life Magazine.*

But by that time, Tempest said, "I'd had it with Portland." She and Johnny sold the Capitol and moved to San Francisco, where they subsequently dissolved their marriage. But that, as Tempest will tell you herself, is another story.

The Tantalizing Candy Renee

BY TODAY'S STANDARDS, the burlesque shows of the '50s were all a bit tame. Dancers usually started fully clothed and worked down to a G-string and pasties. At the time, though, it was hot stuff. There was usually a comedian or tap dancer who did the warm-up. Then the house lights would dim. Down in the pit, the band, consisting of a piano player and drummer would strike up something like "Night Train" as, one by one, the dancers would sashay into the spotlight.

> DANCERS USUALLY STARTED FULLY CLOTHED AND WORKED DOWN TO A G-STRING AND PASTIES. AT THE TIME, THOUGH, IT WAS HOT STUFF.

Like all leg shows, as they were called, the Star had a buzzer system to warn the girls if cops were in the house. The Portland Women's Protective Unit, an all-woman force, regularly sent officers to check out the performances. At the Star, the buzzer went directly from the ticket window in the front to the guy in the projection booth, who could then, in turn, warn the girls via an intercom speaker in the dressing room to keep it clean.

The Star, however, probably had less use for the buzzer these days because the new chief of police, Jim Purcell, had taken a special interest in Candy. On any given night at the Star, you could expect to find Diamond Jim sitting in the third row. It was evident, especially to members of the police force who worked downtown, that Diamond Jim had taken an interest in the Star in general, and Miss Renee in particular, because he'd put out the word that he didn't want any of them backstage.

One night a police officer named Harlon Davis, who moonlighted transporting dancers to and from stag shows, had to enter the forbidden territory to pick up a purse one of the girls had left behind. To his dismay—because he knew he was toast if he was spotted—he saw Candy Renee in the dressing room, her dress half off, talking with the chief.

And then he heard her say: "Shut up, you son of a bitch, and zipper me up." As Davis remembers quite vividly, Purcell did as he was ordered—and Davis took off while the getting was good.

Now, it is entirely possible that Diamond Jim, who fancied himself quite the ladies' man, was simply smitten by the tantalizing charms of Candy Renee. On the other hand, perhaps he was conducting an undercover investigation. At the time, the police bureau was responsible for passing judgment on the moral qualities of Portland entertainment. A board of nine officers—the Censor Board—routinely reviewed all burlesque and stag shows within the city. Police officers had the duty of censoring movies as well. So perhaps Diamond Jim was simply being especially diligent in this regard.

> DAVIS SAW CANDY RENEE IN THE DRESSING ROOM, TALKING WITH THE CHIEF. THEN HE HEARD HER SAY: "SHUT UP, YOU SON OF A BITCH, AND ZIPPER ME UP."

In any case, this seeming idyll came to an abrupt halt one March night in 1954, when Candy and an ex-con by the named of Donald Vance Larson, who happened to work for Jim Elkins, were apprehended on McLoughlin Boulevard after a high-speed chase. There was, first of all, the matter of the drugs that had occasioned the chase in the first place: Candy, sad to say, had a bit of a habit. And then there was the loaded revolver the cops found on the seat between the two lovebirds when they finally stopped the car. According to police records, the two had managed to outrun four squad cars before finally being stopped. Candy, it was noted, was scantily clad.

When all was said and done, Vance was sent back to Washington, from which state he was currently on parole. As for Candy, not even Diamond Jim Purcell could save her after she claimed ownership of the pistol. She had to leave town, too. But we're getting a little ahead of our story.

CANDY RENEE had the police chief's eye.

BUSINESS AS USUAL —WITH A DIFFERENCE

The Startup Cost Was $10,000

IT was back to business as usual, all right, but with one major change. Elkins was running the show now—not the chief of police, and certainly not the bumbling Mayor Peterson. Peterson learned this the hard way.

BART'S DRIVE IN
at 50th and SE Powell

Shortly after he took office, Mayor Peterson got a visit from his pal Swede Ferguson, who wanted to open up an after-hours club in town. This, by the way, is the same Swede Ferguson who just three years earlier had owned and operated the Clover Club, at the corner of Tenth and Taylor, where the offices of the *Willamette Week* are now. This is where Little Rusty and Justice Douglas watched Sammy Davis Jr. performing with the Will Mastin Trio—so it wasn't as though he was just starting out.

ELKINS WAS "THE FIX." IF YOU WANTED TO RUN A GAMBLING OR AFTER-HOURS JOINT OR A HOUSE OF PROSTITUTION, YOU HAD TO GET HIS PERMISSION.

But Ferguson had lost his backing at the Clover Club and now he wanted to open up a new joint—and without having to go through Elkins. So before he did anything else, he stopped by city hall to see his old friend, the mayor, who assured him that everything would be just fine. But no sooner had Swede opened for business than he was raided by the police.

When he was released from custody, Swede got back in touch with the mayor, who told him there must be a misunderstanding somewhere. He'd have a talk with the chief and straighten everything out. When he called in the chief for a little get-together, however, Purcell told Peterson the facts of life: The only way Ferguson could operate was with Elkins's say-so. Eventually, Ferguson was allowed to stay in business—but only after he agreed to give Elkins 75 percent of the take.

Elkins was "the fix." If you wanted to run a gambling or after-hours joint or a house of prostitution, you had to get his permission. The usual start-up cost was $10,000, sometimes $20,000. But he didn't stop there.

ACCORDING TO A OLD ROUNDER named Tony Ricco, one of Elkins's favorite tricks was to contact some madam outside the city and offer her a "perfect location" for about $10,000 down. He would let her operate for about three weeks, then have Lieutenant Crisp, his man on the

ELKINS and his sidekick Ray Clark

vice squad, knock her off. Elkins would then repossess, complaining all the while that he apparently didn't have the control over the police that he thought he had, and start all over again.

Elkins ran the same routine on would-be coin machine operators as well. Harry Huerth, the old safecracker, recalls how out-of-town operators would come to Elkins, wanting to buy in with him. "Then he would sell them the business and say he would fix it with the police so they could operate. The guy would run it for a couple of weeks and then the bulls would come and tell them that the town was too hot. Such and such a church is screaming so you will have to shut down."

After a couple of months, the guy would get wise and try to sell out. But since everyone in town already knew the game, no one would buy. Finally, Elkins would repossess. Huerth says he knew of this happening five or six times.

Under Al Winter, and for decades before that, the payoff had been a well-ordered affair. Everyone understood his place in the scheme of things and knew better than to try to take more than his fair share. But with the mayor and chief of police in his pocket, Elkins didn't have to play by the old rules. In addition to the time-honored payoff, which according to custom was administered by city hall and the police, he instituted his own—with Carl Crisp, lieutenant in charge of the vice squad, as his personal bagman.

THE COST OF DOING any sort of illegal business was going through the roof—and not everyone was liking it.

One day Paul Halperin, who had a little smoke shop downtown at Sixth and Oak and did a little bookmaking on the side, ran into his friend Alfred Battalini at the dog track. Battalini managed the Market Club, over on produce row, for Joe Gatto. "Those dirty bastards," said Battalini, "they want to raise my payoff from $600 to $800 a month." People were complaining all over town.

But if you really wanted to get an earful about the unfairness of it all, the place to go was the Desert Room, where Nate Zusman held forth.

Hot Times at the Desert Room

THE HOT SPOT IN TOWN, now that the Pago Pago and the Turf Club were gone, was the Desert Room, at Southwest Twelfth and Stark. That's the triangular building across from Jake's where the Silverado is now located. The Desert Room was owned by Nate Zusman, a banty rooster of a guy, who called himself the Mark of Stark—in recognition, he would tell you, of the fact that he was a soft touch for anyone who was short a few bucks. Fat chance.

His longtime bartender, Johnnie Bazzutti, said he had to be constantly on guard to keep Zusman from stealing his tips.

Zusman was a thief, a fence, and a pimp—and by all accounts, he ran one of the most fascinating nightclubs Portland has ever seen. On any night of the week, you could expect to find a good portion of the Portland underworld hanging out at the Desert Room. The pimps and madams all made the scene every night, and there was always a contingent of safecrackers, who in those days were considered the princes of the rackets.

> ON ANY NIGHT OF THE WEEK, YOU COULD EXPECT TO FIND A GOOD PORTION OF THE PORTLAND UNDERWORLD HANGING OUT AT THE DESERT ROOM.

That being the case, it only made sense that the intelligence and vice squads camped out there, too—drinking for free, of course—because how else are you going to find out what the other side is up to unless you get to know them? Not too surprisingly, most of the city's politicians and any prosecutor from the DA's office worth his salt could be found there as well, drinking with the boys and taking in the floor shows, which usually featured out-of-town musical acts and some of the finest strippers in town.

Conveniently located across Twelfth Avenue from the Desert Room was the Bellevue Hotel, which was actually a whorehouse run by Blanche Kaye—short for Kazinski, the police records say—a member of one of the city's most successful crime families. The Kayes didn't

like the way things were going now that Elkins was running things, either—taking so much off the top that you were working for hardly more than wages.

Blanche's brother Eddie had connections to the L.A. mob. Another brother, Barney, was the preeminent local bootlegger. He and his wife, Gloria, operated an after-hours club, with a little prostitution on the side, at Seventh and Fremont.

Every week or so, Barney would take off for Reno and come back with the back-seat and trunk of his specially built Cadillac loaded with booze. One night, as he was driving back from Nevada, the State Police stopped him for a broken taillight. Once they saw what he was carrying, they had no choice but to charge him with violating the liquor laws, too. When Barney got back to Portland, he ran into Jim Elkins. "You dumb punk," said Elkins, "don't you know that when you're breaking the law, you don't break the law?"

Good advice at any time, no doubt.

> "YOU DUMB PUNK," ELKINS TOLD BARNEY KAYE, "DON'T YOU KNOW THAT WHEN YOU'RE BREAKING THE LAW, YOU DON'T BREAK THE LAW?"

EDDIE KAYE had connections to the L.A. mob.

The Top Stories of 1953

IN SO MANY WAYS, though, it was a very different world from the one we know today. There were no interstate freeways. No shopping malls. And hard as it is to imagine, no television to speak of. Portland didn't get its first station until late 1952. By the end of 1953, there were only one thousand sets in the metropolitan area.

Dwight Eisenhower was president. A truce accord had been signed that June, bringing to an end the war in Korea. Senator Joseph McCarthy was still on the loose, attempting to rout out Communists—who he seemed to believe had infiltrated the U.S. government. The Cold War was on everybody's minds, raising fears of a nuclear war.

> SENATOR MCCARTHY WAS STILL ON THE LOOSE, ATTEMPTING TO ROUT OUT COMMUNISTS, WHO HE BELIEVED HAD INFILTRATED THE U.S. GOVERNMENT.

A *Journal* story from December 1953 noted that "the city civil defense agency continued pushing plans to make Portlanders as safe as possible in case of an enemy air attack, with the main accomplishment being the completion of preliminary blueprints for an underground control center."

And if that didn't set you entirely at ease, it should be noted that once the underground center was completed, the man in charge of it would be Portland's new mayor, Fred Peterson, who as the year ended, issued a statement noting the accomplishments of his first year in office.

During 1953, Peterson noted, the city council, with himself at the helm, had voted to place three important measures on the ballot for the next spring: a waterfront improvement measure, an $8 million bond issue for a new sports center, and a much-needed expansion of the zoo in Washington Park. As Portlanders were well aware, that year the zoo had received its first elephant, a young female from Thailand named Rosy.

FILL 'ER UP at Rogers Union Service.

◄ *THE ROSE CITY,* circa 1954.

▲ *PARKING*, the modern way.

▲ *At THE CORNER OF* 4th and Washington.

► **THE ROSE QUEEN** and her court.

HAMBURGER EATING CONTEST at the Speck Drive-In.

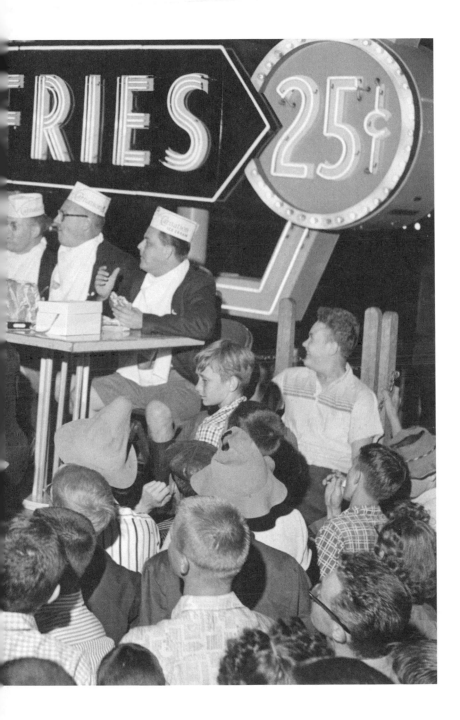

"I am encouraged with the year's accomplishments," said the mayor, "But I wouldn't say I'm satisfied, for I am never satisfied. Having been in business as long as I have, I know you can't stand still. You either have to go forward or backward, and I don't intend to go backward."

The *Oregonian's* pick for top local news story of the year was the State Milk Control Board's decision to raise the price of milk a penny, to twenty-three cents a quart. "The meeting," said the story, "had not been publicized, the reasons for the ordered increase were not made clear. The *Oregonian* was a leader in the furor that resulted."

The Academy Award for best movie of the year went to the World War II drama *From Here to Eternity,* with Burt Lancaster and Deborah Kerr embracing in the surf at Waikiki. *How to Marry a Millionaire,* with Marilyn Monroe, in Cinemascope, was playing at the big theaters downtown.

Newspaper ads said that if you acted right away you could get a new twenty-one-inch Tele-King table model television—$130 off the regular price—at just $199.95. Bargain hunters should be warned, however. That would be $1,348 in today's money.

At Thriftway you could get three cans of Franco-American spaghetti for thirty-five cents.

IT WAS THE AGE OF TWO-MARTINI LUNCHES. EVERYONE SMOKED CIGARETTES. BUSINESSMEN WORE HATS. WOMEN DIDN'T WEAR SLACKS DOWNTOWN.

Noting that the Oregon Legislature had just that spring passed a law allowing liquor by the drink, the *Journal* dubbed 1953 the "Year of the Cocktail." Even then, thanks to the State Liquor Commission's efforts to keep prices up, there was still plenty of work for Barney Kaye and the rest of Portland's bootleggers.

It was the age of two-martini lunches. Everyone smoked cigarettes. Businessmen wore hats. Women didn't wear slacks downtown. When they dressed up, they wore gloves.

High school kids stopped at drive-ins like the Tik Tok on Sandy for a hamburger and a Coke—fifty cents.

Les Paul and Mary Ford sang "Vaya Con Dios."

The pert Patti Page had a big hit on her hands with "How Much Is That Doggie in the Window."

OH, YES. One more thing about Portland back then. It was still one of the most rigidly segregated cities north of the Mason-Dixon Line.

In 1952, two black couples were denied entry to a public dance at Jantzen Beach until the leader of the orchestra, Lionel Hampton, refused to go on with the show.

Oregon didn't pass open housing legislation until 1953. Later the same year, there was a cross-burning in the yard of a black family that had moved into the middle-class Parkrose district. There were still "Whites Only" signs in some Portland restaurants.

> AND ONE MORE THING: PORTLAND WAS STILL ONE OF THE MOST RIGIDLY SEGREGATED CITIES NORTH OF THE MASON-DIXON LINE.

With a history like that, it only stands to reason that there was an exclusively black part of town, with its own shops and clubs, its own music, and its own rackets—which, it only stands to reason, were protected like those in every other part of town.

Welcome to the Avenue

JOHN ROE had been on the vice squad just a few days when he struck up a conversation with a hooker at Paul's Paradise, a club just off Williams Avenue in what was then the black part of town. After a few minutes, the young woman, who of course didn't know that Roe was a cop, because he wasn't in uniform, suggested they continue the conversation at a nearby house. Seeing a chance to jump-start his career, Roe concurred.

As soon as she opened the door, Roe could see that the house was a full-service vice operation, with booze and gambling on the first floor. But there was no reason to hurry. Upstairs, he waited until the woman asked for money and made the arrest. Then he went back downstairs and arrested everybody else. A tall, thin black man who seemed to be in charge asked if he could make a phone call. "Why not?" said Roe. The man dialed a number, spoke with someone for several minutes, then held out the phone to Roe. "Here," he said, "your commander wants to talk with you." Roe took the phone. "Whaddya think you're doing?" said a familiar voice. "Get out of there."

> BIRD HELD OUT THE PHONE TO ROE. "WHADDYA THINK YOU'RE DOING?" SAID ROE'S COMMANDER. "GET OUT OF THERE."

Welcome to the Avenue. It's gone now, for the most part—destroyed to make way for sports complexes and overhead freeways. But once upon a time, it was a bustling community, stretching out along Williams Avenue, from the river, where the Coliseum and Rose Garden are now, up to about Russell—with its own shops and clubs, and of course, its own rackets, paying protection money to the police and city hall.

And that smooth-talking gentleman who introduced Roe to his commanding officer on that long-ago excursion onto the Avenue? That was Birches Bird, right-hand man to Tom Johnson, the boss of the Avenue himself. Bird, a relative newcomer to Portland, had shot and killed a man back in Kansas City. Once in prison, however, his talents were quickly recognized and he was assigned to the governor's mansion as the governor's personal valet, a job which he faithfully executed until his early release from prison and subsequent migration to Portland.

TOM JOHNSON ran the rackets on the Avenue.

But if Bird had led a remarkable life, he didn't hold a candle to Tom Johnson. Johnson, a highly successful businessman reputed to be worth millions, owned a real estate agency, the Keystone Investment Co., which was situated in a large brick building on North Williams, about a hundred yards north of where the Rose Garden is today.

HOT TIMES at Li'l Sandy's on Williams Avenue.

He sold real estate, all right. He had a corner on the blacks-only neighborhoods. Only a few people knew that he was also active in the white parts of town, buying and selling through Emanuel Green,

Portland Challenger

BILL HILLIARD, seated, published the *Challenger.*

a man of African and Jewish heritage who, to use the expression of that time, could "pass" for white.

Real estate, however, was only one of Tom Johnson's business interests. In the rear of the Keystone was a gambling and after-hours club—just one of several illegal enterprises Johnson had a piece of on the Avenue and elsewhere. In the basement of the Keystone was an eight-foot-square safe filled with stacks of hundred-dollar bills.

Born in 1888 to parents who had been plantation slaves, Tom Johnson had grown up in Texas. When his oldest brother was murdered by the Ku Klux Klan—according to family lore, they tied him to the railroad tracks and let a train run over him—young Tom left Texas and worked as a gandy dancer on the railroad, eventually ending up in Portland, where he got into the bootlegging business.

The policeman, John Roe, who later became good friends with both Bird and Johnson, says Tom Johnson told him he actually got his start transporting whiskey from Canada for the Ku Klux Klan, which was at one time powerful in Portland. If this seems a bit contradictory, all you have to keep in mind is that Tom Johnson knew the color of money, and it was green.

There was another side of Johnson, which Bill Hilliard—then a twenty-six-year-old crusading journalist, with a newspaper of his own on Williams Avenue—saw once or twice. Hilliard, who called his paper the *Challenger,* focused on the civil rights struggle, which was then beginning to grip Portland as well as the rest of the nation. Tom Johnson regularly bought an ad for the Keystone Investment Company in Hilliard's paper.

From time to time, Hilliard would take time out from civil rights to write editorials denouncing "vice and corruption" in the black part of town. "And you know," recalls Hilliard, "the next day, Old Tom would come in and take out another ad. I think he was kind of proud of us."
Tom Johnson's grandniece, Rochelle Henninger, who visited him as a girl at his three-story house on Northeast San Rafael Street, recalls that he had servants and served caviar on ordinary occasions. He had a yacht on the Columbia, and a ranch in Eastern Oregon where he raised Arabian horses. At the close of each visit, she says, he would hand her a fifty- or hundred-dollar bill and tell her that money was power. Coming from Tom Johnson, this was not idle chatter.

POLITICS AND THE PINBALL WARS

Sheriff Elliott Had a Problem

IF the city of Portland had a well-developed payoff system, so did the county. The payoff there went through an old bootlegger named Stan Terry, who was by now Elkins's chief rival in the coin machine business.

Back in 1948, with Dorothy McCullough Lee a shoo-in for mayor, Elkins, Terry, and the other gambling interests had managed to elect a candidate to their liking as county sheriff. Mike Elliott, a genial deputy sheriff of no particular distinction up to that point, had campaigned on the strength of his record as a Marine war hero and former University of Michigan football player. As Elliott would later reveal, he also profited from the sage media advice of Elkins himself.

"Right after the primary," Elliott would later say, "I heard from Elkins. He congratulated me and said he would take care of my campaign expenses. He never believed, however, that I would be elected, and the money he donated was very little. He did, however, give me some help for newspaper publicity. He told me that slot machines were in the Three Star Tavern, a spot owned by Stan Terry, and suggested I make a citizen's arrest.

"I went out to the Three Star, found the slot machines, then called the police for the raid. It worked out real fine and I got a good spread. A short time later Elkins told me of another Stan Terry spot—a tavern on 82nd Street—and I pulled another citizen's arrest there where the machines were confiscated."

> "I WENT OUT TO THE THREE STAR, FOUND THE SLOT MACHINES, THEN CALLED THE POLICE FOR THE RAID. A SHORT TIME LATER ELKINS TOLD ME OF ANOTHER STAN TERRY SPOT."

Unfortunately for all concerned, soon after the election, it was revealed in the newspapers that Elliott was not only *not* a Marine hero but had been kicked out of the Marines before the war even started. Nor, for that matter, had he ever attended the University of Michigan, as a football player or anything else. In fact, he had dropped out of school after the tenth grade. But if Elliott was embarrassed, he didn't show it, turning aside all suggestions that he resign.

Several months after the election, Elkins called up Elliott and told him there was a big game that night at the El Rancho Village, at about

MIKE ELLIOTT ran for sheriff—and won.

127th and Stark, and that Elliott, as the sheriff of Multnomah County, should knock it off.

> "THE NEXT DAY I CALLED UP ELKINS AND ASKED HIM WHAT HE WAS TRYING TO PULL. ELKINS LAUGHED AND SAID, 'I GUESS THAT WILL PULL THE GRAFTING SONS OF BITCHES INTO LINE.'"

"I gathered up 19 detectives and went out to raid the place. It was loaded with all the top brass of the Portland Police Department except Purcell. What I had hit was an International Footprinters Association stag party." The Footprinters was a fraternal police organization. "The next day I called up Elkins and asked him what he was trying to pull. Elkins laughed and said, 'I guess that will pull the grafting sons of bitches into line.'"

THE WHEELS DIDN'T actually fall off the sheriff's wagon, however, until several months later, when the *Oregonian*'s star police reporter, Wally Turner, acting on a tip by Jim Elkins himself, discovered Elliott vacationing with a couple of hookers in Nevada. Turner says Elkins trusted him because he had once turned down a bribe. The story appeared in the paper, and this time—you'd better believe it—that was enough for the citizens of Portland, who promptly drummed Elliott out of office in a recall election.

Exactly why Elkins, who had Elliott exactly where he wanted him, would do such a thing, we'll never know. Perhaps it was just another expression of what seems to have been Elkins's particularly wry sense of humor. But whatever it was, the removal of Elliott would have unpredictably dire consequences—for now, the County Commissioners, over whom Elkins had virtually no influence, would choose the next sheriff. At the insistence of the local Democratic Party, they named a young and personable captain in the Fire Department by the name of Terry Schrunk.

Schrunk, a hard-drinking, skirt-chasing sort of guy, might have been a little naive by Portland political standards, but that didn't matter, because Ray Kell did his thinking for him. Kell, a sharp downtown lawyer who represented pinball interests, was the former law partner

STAN TERRY, pinball magnate.

of Gus Solomon, who had just been appointed a federal judge. Solomon was, in turn, a good friend of Al Winter.

According to a police informant, the payoff to the County Commission for making Schrunk the new sheriff was $10,000, and was made by the Teamsters, a new force in Oregon politics. One of the commissioners, Ralph Gleason, raised a ruckus because he was paid his share in $100 bills—which, as he rightly complained, were too big to spend in Portland without drawing attention to himself. Clearly, life as a public servant has never been a bed of roses.

Let the Pinball Wars Begin

THE PINBALL WARS were unrelenting. Elkins's goons raided clubs that had Stan Terry's machines. Sometimes they'd pull their guns and steal the operators' hard-earned cash. Sometimes they'd just steal the machines. But no matter what Elkins tries, Terry just won't go away. In fact, he seems to be gaining.

> ELKINS'S GOONS RAIDED CLUBS THAT HAD STAN TERRY'S MACHINES. NO MATTER WHAT ELKINS TRIES, TERRY JUST WON'T GO AWAY. IN FACT, HE SEEMS TO BE GAINING.

Elkins goes to Seattle to see if he can work out something with the Teamsters. Elkins understands the Teamsters. They're crooks just like he is. From reading the papers, he knows they've used their muscle to take over the coin machine businesses back east. Elkins wants them to do the same thing in Portland.

Try as he might, Elkins can't get through to Teamster boss Frank Brewster. He doesn't have the juice. However, he does get introduced to a short, fat, ex-pimp and racetrack tout by the name of Tom Maloney—Blubber Maloney, as everyone calls him—which is just about as good. Like any self-respecting Seattle hood, Maloney has a few Teamster connections. Mostly, though, he's tight with Frank Colacurcio, whose family runs the Seattle mob.

Before long Maloney is in Portland, running the campaign for Elkins's candidate for district attorney, William Langley. Langley, the scion of a prominent West Hills family and amateur golf champion, is a bit of a fool, which suits Elkins just fine.

Elkins has actually done a little business with him. Several years earlier, when Langley was in private practice, he invested $10,000 in one of Elkins's gambling joints called the China Lantern. Elkins immediately fleeced him of the money by running in a dealer who lost the entire $10,000 to one of Elkins's confederates. The fact that Langley will even talk to him now is further proof of his gullibility. For obvious reasons, Elkins considers it vitally important to have his man in the DA's office.

STAN TERRY holds a news conference to promote his petition to legalize pinball.

But even now, before the election, Elkins, Maloney, and the district-attorney-to-be are busy making plans in Maloney's room at the Roosevelt Hotel on Southwest Park.

It couldn't be much simpler. They'll set up a pinball owners' organization affiliated with the Teamsters. If you're a member, the Teamsters will do business with any place that has your machines. If you're not, they'll shut the place down. And here's the kicker: Stan Terry won't be allowed to join.

> IT COULDN'T BE MUCH SIMPLER. IF YOU'RE A MEMBER, THE TEAMSTERS WILL DO BUSINESS WITH ANY PLACE THAT HAS YOUR MACHINES. IF YOU'RE NOT, THEY'LL SHUT THE PLACE DOWN.

Maloney, who's always bragging about his Teamster connections, says he'll walk to Seattle on his knees if it doesn't work.

But before any of this can come to pass, of course, they have to get Langley elected. Like every candidate, Langley needs an issue that will capture the imagination of the voting public. Since there are no records of their deliberations, we can only imagine the lofty discussions that took place before the three of them arrived at a solution: Langley would accuse the incumbent, John McCourt, of being soft on crime.

It is, of course, a brilliant solution—not because it is anywhere near original, but because it always works. Not only that, they already have at their disposal the very case they need to drive home the point.

Earlier that year, a severely decayed body had been found by the side of a country road near Washougal, Washington, wrapped in blankets tied together by ropes. It was quickly identified as that of Diane Hank, a sixteen-year-old Lincoln High School student, last seen drinking martinis at the Portland home of Wayne Fong and his wife, Sherry, one night about two months before.

After Diane had failed to show up at school the next morning, the Fongs had been hauled in for questioning and then released. It didn't look good for the Fongs—but as most authorities quickly realized, that didn't make them guilty of murder.

In fact, as an analysis of her remains would later establish beyond a reasonable doubt, Diane had died from an overdose of alcohol and barbiturates—a combination that was popular with the hipster underworld at that time. Diane had apparently just overdone it that night.

After examining the evidence, the district attorney, John McCourt, found no evidence that the teenager's death had been anything but an accident. In addition, there was no apparent motive. Diane, who frequently baby-sat for the Fongs' two young children, was a good friend of Sherry Fong's.

And there the sad case of Diane Hank might have rested had it

BLUBBER MALONEY bragged about Teamster connections.

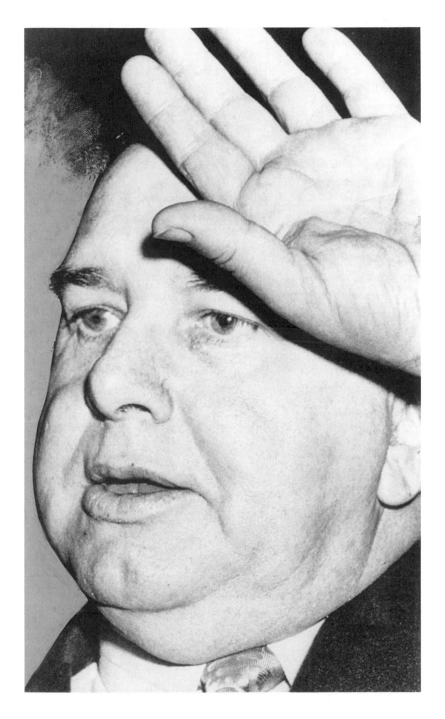

not been the political season in Portland. The incumbent, Langley charged, was guilty of "dereliction of duty" for failing to bring murder indictments against the Fongs. As even Langley had to know, this was pure bunk.

TO GIVE LANGLEY his due, there were indeed certain aspects of the Fong case that would raise anyone's eyebrows. In the first place, the Fongs were an interracial couple. Fong was Chinese, his wife, Sherry, was Caucasian. That sort of thing was frowned upon in those days.

In addition, Fong was clearly not a reputable character. He'd already spent a few months in McNeil Island on a federal narcotics rap. Clearly, something scandalous was going on at the Fong place.

There were problems with Fong's story as well. For starters, if it was a simple matter of an accidental overdose, why hadn't the Fongs just called a doctor? Or, when worse came to worst, at least reported her death to the proper authorities?

Well, as it happened, the Fongs, or more specifically, Wayne, had a problem: Wayne Fong was one of Portland's major drug dealers. After his release from prison, Fong had returned to Portland to resume his duties with an organization, based in the Sun Sang Restaurant, located kitty-corner from the police headquarters at Second and Oak, that dispensed high-grade Chinese white heroin to the junkies of Portland. Although the group enjoyed the protection of the local police, it is perfectly understandable that the Fongs might not have wanted to draw attention to the body of a dead girl who had OD'd in their living room.

> IT IS UNDERSTANDABLE THAT THE FONGS MIGHT NOT HAVE WANTED TO DRAW ATTENTION TO THE BODY OF A DEAD GIRL WHO HAD OD'D IN THEIR LIVING ROOM.

When you got right down to it, that didn't make the Fongs guilty of murder. But that was just a distressing technicality that Langley would have to wrestle with once he became district attorney of Multnomah County.

With Maloney as his campaign manager, the Fong case as a campaign

BILL LANGLEY, the new DA, was all for law and order.

issue, and the Teamsters and the Portland underworld paying the bulk of the campaign bills, Langley wins the election, taking office in January 1955.

LANGLEY HAS HARDLY been in office two months when the Teamsters throw a picket line around the Mt. Hood Café, which is where all the Radio Cab drivers go to play pinball. It is no accident that all the pinball machines there belong to Stan Terry. The Teamsters don't have anything against the owner, Old Man Crouch. But now, unless Terry removes his machines, nothing—no food, no beer, no nothing—can be delivered. Crouch will be out of business. It looks like the end for Terry.

OREGON JOURNAL

ed, Controlled, Edited

TELEPHONE CApitol 5511

PRICE 15 CENTS

ON, SUNDAY, FEB. 28, 1954

Her Death Puzzling

BODY of Diane Agnes Hank, 16-year-old Lincoln high school student, was found in Clark county, Washington, giving detectives second mystery death to solve in week's time.

Police Hold 3 In Mysterious Death of Girl

Police Saturday night booked three persons who had been under questioning about the death of Diane Agnes Hank, 16-year-old Lincoln high school student, whose decomposed body was found tied in a blanket near Washougal, Wash., seven weeks after she was reported missing.

Wey Hin (Wayne) Fong, 25, of 3405 SW Barbur boulevard, was booked on a charge of disregarding a traffic signal, violation of the after-hours ordinance and investigation, with bail set at $510 by city authorities. He is held on an additional charge of contributing to the delinquency of a minor, with bail set at $10,000 by District Attorney John B. McCourt.

THE MAN'S wife, Mrs. Marjorie L. (Sherry) Fong, 22, also was booked on a contributing charge by the district attorney, with bail at $10,000. Another man, Kwong Tjng Yee, 28, identified as a frequent house guest of the Fongs, was held on an after-hours charge, for investigation and for immigration authorities, with bail at $500. Police said he is a native of China.

After an autopsy, pathologists Saturday night were unable to explain the death of the 16-year-old Hank girl, whose bound body was found wrapped in bedding Friday afternoon along the Evergreen highway near the east limit of Clark county, Wash-

Rebels Resign

ia, Feb. 27.— Adib Shishekly d on rioting ich were not esignation as anded the unessor, too. Six-persons were injured. ng could be ter of the city, rnment buildre Jo municipal

street fighting in several other city. oldiers used tear ousands of demroamed the city re the shooting

disorders some of ke into the paring and beat up

L Syrian army ofaged Friday's revoAleppo and other

▶ **WAYNE FONG,** heroin dealer.

U. S. PENITENTIARY
ALCATRAZ
1562
4 29 62

Elkins doesn't even have time to celebrate. Terry goes to see a local moneylender named Karl Shear, who handles some of the syndicate's money-laundering activities in Portland. Lester Beckman, the slot machine king under Al Winter and just out of McNeil Island, gets involved in this, too, as Terry is escorted down to Las Vegas to talk to a guy named Hy Goldbaum.

Interesting fellow, this Hy Goldbaum: pit boss for the Flamingo, which is, of course, the syndicate-controlled casino started by Bugsy Siegel. Siegel, of course, is no longer around to oversee its operation, having been murdered in 1947 on the orders of Meyer Lansky, after he discovered Siegel taking a little money off the top—skimming the skim, as it were. Goldbaum, as he would later testify, is also a bill collector for the casino.

> A LITTLE CASH—MAYBE $10,000—CHANGES HANDS. AND JUST LIKE THAT, IT'S OVER. THE PICKET IS LIFTED AT THE MT. HOOD CAFÉ. ELKINS IS EFFECTIVELY OUT OF THE PINBALL BUSINESS.

So Goldbaum takes Stan Terry up to Seattle, walks him into the office of Teamster boss Frank Brewster. A little cash—maybe $10,000—changes hands. And just like that, it's over. The picket is lifted at the Mt. Hood Café. A few months later, Elkins sells his pinball routes to Terry. Elkins is effectively out of the lucrative pinball business.

It's the Same Old Scam

AS MUST BE PAINFULLY obvious by now, Maloney just doesn't have the juice with the Teamsters that he said he did. If anything, the Teamsters are now lined up against Elkins. But Elkins didn't get where he is by feeling sorry for himself.

As a reward for Maloney's admittedly imperfect efforts on his behalf, Elkins offers him a piece of the action—a chance to buy into the Portland rackets. Naturally, Maloney doesn't have any money himself, but he knows someone who does.

His friend Frank Colacurcio, whose family runs the rackets in Seattle, takes a room at the Roosevelt Hotel, and opens negotiations with Elkins. He wants to set up three or four houses of prostitution in Portland, and he's willing to pay for the privilege. But he's wise to Elkins, so he won't give Elkins any money up front. Instead, he offers Elkins a share of the proceeds. Elkins turns him down. Colacurcio throws up his hands and goes back to Seattle.

But Maloney, whatever his faults, is not easily discouraged, either. He contacts an acquaintance, a fellow by the name of Joe McLaughlin. McLaughlin, a former card room operator in Seattle, is looking for a score. McLaughlin shows up in Portland and joins the deliberations at the Roosevelt Hotel.

THE DESERT ROOM, a downtown hangout for hookers, pimps, safecrackers, and of course, the vice squad.

THEY DIDN'T call her Big Helen for nothing.

It's the same old scam. Except that this time, instead of charging his usual ten or twenty grand, Elkins gets McLaughlin to pony up $50,000.

At Maloney and McLaughlin's request, Elkins arranges for two downtown billiard parlors, the Rialto and the Elite, to provide poker and dice games. Then, after a couple of weeks, he has Crisp and his boys close them both down.

> IT'S THE SAME OLD SCAM. EXCEPT THAT THIS TIME, INSTEAD OF CHARGING HIS USUAL TEN OR TWENTY GRAND, ELKINS GETS MCLAUGHLIN TO PONY UP $50,000.

Maloney and McLaughlin meet with similar success when they request Elkins's assistance in setting up a new whorehouse. They go so far as to bring in a madam from Seattle by the name of Ann Thompson. Elkins meets her at the airport and tells her that, regrettably, prospects are not good. The police, he says, simply won't allow any more prostitution in Portland.

By now, it's beginning to dawn on Maloney and McLaughlin that Elkins has been sandbagging them. They start looking around for someone else to make the Portland connections for them—and they find him in the person of Nate Zusman, proprietor of the Desert Room.

Zusman, who has aspirations of replacing Elkins as the "fix" in Portland, is nothing if not agreeable. He informs a couple of ladies who frequent the Desert Room, Helen Hardy and Helen Smalley—Big and Little Helen, as they are called—that he has the assurances of the district attorney's campaign manager, Blubber Maloney himself, that the DA does not object to the opening of a new call girl operation in town. Not long afterward, Big and Little Helen open for business on Northwest Pettygrove.

When Elkins hears about the new whorehouse, he has the police shut it down. This time, the chief himself, Diamond Jim Purcell, leads the raid.

Elkins has won the skirmish, but unless he does something quick, he knows he's in danger of losing much, much more.

Maloney Checks in at the King

WHAT JIM ELKINS now knows for sure is that Blubber Maloney is scheming behind his back to set up the town. What he doesn't know is what that big, fat blowhard is going to try next, and he figures he'd better find out before it's too late. But how?

One day in the summer of 1955, what can only be understood as Providence drops a little present in Elkins's lap: Maloney is being kicked out of his room at the Roosevelt Hotel. Nearly half a century later, we really don't know why. All the principals in this little drama are dead, and not even the old vice cop, the one who saw it all, can recall. For all we know, Elkins might have engineered it himself. Certainly, he was capable of it.

In any case, the next time Elkins sees Maloney, he tells him he knows of a nice, quiet place that might be just the ticket. According to his best information, the King Tower, that spanking new twelve-story tower at the foot of the city's West Hills, has a vacancy: all the modern appliances, great view, everything you could ask for.

> THE NEXT TIME ELKINS SEES MALONEY, HE TELLS HIM HE KNOWS OF A NICE, QUIET PLACE. THE ONLY THING ELKINS FORGETS TO TELL HIM IS THAT THE ROOM IS BUGGED.

Maloney checks it out and finds that for once, at least, Elkins is telling him the truth. He takes the King's one remaining vacancy, room 503.

About the only thing Elkins forgets to tell him is that the room is bugged—and operating the recording machine next door is Elkins's lieutenant Ray Clark, as likeable a scalawag as you're likely to meet in this or any other story. Once number-two man on the vice squad, he's a civilian now and married to Gerry Rogers, one of Portland's leading madams.

It's worse than Elkins thought. As he listens to the tapes, he can hear Maloney, McLaughlin, and Langley plotting to divvy up the Portland rackets—and without him. Langley even talks about setting up Elkins—whom they call "the character"—for a fall. And Maloney's in the middle of everything.

Elkins's first thought, of course, is to try to blackmail Langley, now the sitting district attorney. Langley calls Elkins's bluff. The tapes are at least as damaging to Elkins as anyone else.

Shut down there, Elkins figures he'll take one more shot at getting Brewster, the regional Teamsters boss in Seattle, to straighten things out. Anything to get Maloney off his back. Last time, Elkins couldn't even get through to Brewster. He's wiser now. He's seen how Stan Terry did it over the Mt. Hood Café deal. Maybe it'll work for him, too. So Elkins goes to Lester Beckman, the slot machine king with connections to the national syndicate. Beckman takes him to Las Vegas to meet with Flamingo pit boss Hy Goldbaum. Goldbaum takes him up to Seattle. Brewster tells Elkins to pound sand. Maloney's not his boy, anyway, he's Colacurcio's.

It's looking bad, but whatever else you might think of Elkins, he's not a quitter. It just so happens that he has something in mind for a new acquaintance of his: one Herman "Bugsy" Burns, not to be confused with Bugsy Siegel, after whom Burns is probably trying to model himself.

> ELKINS HAS SOMETHING MORE DEMANDING IN MIND. HE ASKS BURNS FOR HIS PROFESSIONAL ADVICE ON HOW TO DISPOSE OF A BODY.

And while not in the same class as the original Bugsy, Burns, who's just out of the Washington State Pen in Walla Walla, is a tough cookie in his own right. Elkins has been using him to pick up and deliver heroin from a source in Seattle. This time, however, Elkins has something more demanding in mind. He asks Burns for his professional advice on how to dispose of a body. No need to ask who Elkins has in mind.

Burns tells Elkins something he picked up working for the mob down in Miami. First, you find yourself an open grave where they're going to bury someone the next day. Then you dig down another three or four feet and throw the stiff in there. Then you fill it back up. Usually you're going to have some dirt left over, so you need a tarpaulin to carry the excess dirt away. That way, it's a whole lot easier.

A Job for Bugsy Burns

ON A SEPTEMBER evening in 1955, two of Lieutenant Crisp's toughest guys grab Maloney as he's coming out of the King Tower and take him for a little ride up through the West Hills to Cornell Road. They pull over when they come to a secluded spot.

One of the cops is sitting in the backseat next to Maloney. The one driving takes out his gun and turns around: "This a good place?"

Somehow, the rear car door next to Maloney has been left ajar. Maloney sees it and seizes the opportunity. He pushes the door open and races away down the hill. The cops, who never intended to do anything more than scare the daylights out of him anyway, can't stop laughing. "For a little fat guy," as one of them recalls today, "he sure could run."

When Maloney gets back to the King Tower, he throws everything in his car, then drives down to Second and Oak where he spends the rest of the night parked in front of police headquarters. If they're going to kill him, he later testifies, they'll have to do it in front of the police station. The next morning Blubber Maloney leaves town, heading, although of course nobody else knows it at the time, straight for Seattle mob boss Frank Colacurcio's vacation retreat at Hayden Lake, Idaho.

As things work out, Elkins never gets the chance to use Bugsy Burns's ingenious burial scheme. Clearly, however, he is impressed with the man's abilities. The next time Burns is in town, Elkins tells him to bring a couple of his friends from Walla Walla. Now that Maloney's gone, Elkins can turn his full attention to the Stan Terry problem.

The plan, as Elkins explains it, is for them to pose as pinball repairmen and steal all of Terry's machines. He's already got fake IDs for them. He's got the trucks. They should be able to hit every joint that uses Terry's machines in a single day. Each place they stop, they'll tell the owner they're taking his outdated machines and replacing them with new ones. Another truck with new ones will be along in an hour or so. If they work fast, they'll be done before anyone figures out

HERMAN "BUGSY" BURNS

what's happened. Elkins already has a warehouse where they can hide them set aside on Williams Avenue.

It is a shockingly brilliant plan. In one fell swoop, Elkins who, it will be remembered, had to sell his machines to Terry after the fiasco at the Mt. Hood Café, will be back in the coin machine business. And who knows, it might even have worked, if only Bugsy and the boys—

BAIL BONDSMEN set up shop across from the police station.

apparently finding themselves with too much time on their hands, as they waited for the go-ahead from Elkins—hadn't first got caught holding up the Safeway on Northeast Broadway and sent to the Oregon State Pen. As ever, good help is so hard to find.

CAR BOMBING at the country club.

BURNING ISSUES OF THE DAY

"Who Do You Think's Running It?"

IT'S the fall of 1955 and there's a virtual mob war going on in Portland. So where, you might well ask, is the press, that watchdog of democracy?

Well, rest assured that at least one member of the Fourth Estate, James Burr Miller of the

Oregonian, is onto the scent—and if he doesn't exactly suspect the titanic struggle taking place between the city and county machines for control of the Portland payoff, at least he's got an inkling that the payoff exists in the first place.

Miller, who is twenty-seven years old, has recently been assigned to cover the police beat for his paper. He's heard rumors of the payoff before, but until one fateful day in September, when he bumps into

JAMES BURR MILLER, *Oregonian* cub reporter.

Jack Olsen in the second-floor hallway of the police station, that's all they are—just rumors.

Olsen, a bright young officer, actually just a year younger than Miller, is upset. When Miller asks him why, he says he's been offered a bribe. Just a few dollars, mind you, but a bribe nevertheless. It appears that officers on his new beat—the Avenue—routinely accept money from neighborhood racketeers in exchange for looking the other way.

What's more, when he'd objected, suggesting to his partner that maybe someone should tell their superiors about it, his partner had scoffed at him: "Who do you think's running it, anyway?"

Olsen says he's going to seek a transfer, but Miller talks him out of it. Since it's probably going to be the same anyplace else, he says, why not stay on and document the criminal wrongdoing? Olsen agrees to start keeping records of the payoff money he receives—in effect, conducting an undercover operation against the Portland Police Bureau. It's not exactly what Olsen had in mind when he joined the force a year ago, number one in his recruiting class, but he doesn't know what else to do.

> IT'S NOT EXACTLY WHAT OLSEN HAD IN MIND WHEN HE JOINED THE FORCE A YEAR AGO, NUMBER ONE IN HIS RECRUITING CLASS, BUT HE DOESN'T KNOW WHAT ELSE TO DO.

There are five places along Olsen's beat that make the monthly payoff. Four of them are gambling operations—the main one being Tom Johnson's Keystone Club at the corner of Williams and Cherry—and the fifth is a bawdy house at 1420 Larrabee. Each one pays $10-20 a month to every cop who walks the beat. Every time Olsen gets his cut, he dutifully records the event, right down to the serial numbers of the bills he receives.

It isn't much. But the plan is to work their way up the ladder to the big boys. And when they've accumulated enough damning evidence, Miller will write the exposé that'll bring down the whole corrupt system.

What they don't understand is that there are two payoffs. The big one, collected each month by the precinct captains, then distributed to their superiors at police headquarters and city hall, is the prize, worth hundreds of thousands of dollars annually—millions in today's dollars—that makes the wheels of city government go 'round.

The other payoff, the one that they've stumbled onto, involves the small monthly stipends of $10 or $20—smile money—collected by beat officers. The two are really quite separate.

If Olsen and Miller had understood this, perhaps they wouldn't have gone to all the trouble. On the other hand, maybe it wouldn't have changed anything. Official corruption is, after all, official corruption—and, as already noted, they were both quite young.

You Could Wake up in the River

WITHOUT DIVULGING the name of his contact in the Police Bureau, Miller tells his editors about the plan. Out of what might be construed as prudence, they tell Miller to get the okay of the county's top law enforcement official, district attorney Bill Langley, before going any further.

Langley listens politely, but declines to offer any assistance—not too surprisingly, since he is at that moment deeply involved in an attempt to seize control of the payoff system. He simply doesn't have the manpower to devote to such a task, he says. But at least Miller now has his editor's permission to proceed.

Word of Miller's project soon leaks out. The chief, Diamond Jim Purcell himself, suddenly becomes quite friendly, offering Miller his assistance in the investigation. When Miller refuses to tell him who his undercover source is, Captain Bob Mariels—whose wife, if Miller only knew, operates a bootlegging establishment out of their home—drops by to offer Miller a membership in the Footprinters Society.

The Footprinters, you'll remember, is that fraternal order of law enforcement professionals who meet once a month to get drunk and

OFFICER JACK OLSEN, our man on the Avenue.

JACK F. OLSE

watch stag shows. Miller declines Mariels's kind offer, saying he doesn't have enough money to join.

The vice squad puts a tail on Miller, but they can't figure out who he's been talking to. Miller and Olsen are too smart. They call each other from phone booths. They meet in out-of-the-way places, entering department stores by one entrance and leaving by another to throw off anyone who might be following.

Mariels comes back. He's found a sponsor willing to underwrite the Footprinters membership fee. But first, Mariels says, the sponsor would like to meet with him—just to get to know him better, you understand. Miller says sure.

Mariels sets up a meeting in the cocktail lounge of the Multnomah Hotel, now the Embassy Suites, on Southwest Pine. When Miller and Mariels arrive, who should be sitting at the table but Jim Elkins. Miller recognizes Elkins, who he knows is supposed to be the mob boss of Portland. After a few minutes of chitchat, Mariels leaves Miller and Elkins alone in the dimly lit lounge. Elkins leans forward across the table.

"This is for the club," he says. Miller can still remember his gravelly voice and the touch of something under the table. It's an envelope with a thick wad of bills.

> "YOU'RE IN A VERY INTERESTING PROFESSION," MILLER SAYS, TRYING TO BE CLEVER. "WHO KNOWS, I MIGHT HAVE TO ACCEPT AN ASSIGNMENT TO WRITE ABOUT YOU SOME DAY."

Miller says he can't accept the money. He's a reporter, after all.

"You're in a very interesting profession," Miller says, trying to be clever. "Who knows, I might have to accept an assignment to write about you some day."

Elkins sits back.

"Anyone who would do that would not be very smart," he says very slowly. "Accidents happen. You could fall and hit your head and wake up in the river. Or there could be a fire. You're a family man. You have children. Sometimes houses catch fire during the night and everyone is killed. Do you understand what I mean?"

Diane Hank "Knew Too Much"

IT'S LATE FALL OF 1955. The town is in the grips of a sociopath. The Rose City is about to explode in a parox-ysm of shameful headlines and, ultimately, the airing of its dirty laundry on national television. But even if, somehow, the good people of Portland had an inkling of what was about to befall them, it's even money that they would still have pursued, just as avidly, the burning issues of the day.

> THE ROSE CITY IS ABOUT TO EXPLODE IN A PAROXYSM OF SHAMEFUL HEADLINES AND, ULTIMATELY, THE AIRING OF ITS DIRTY LAUNDRY ON NATIONAL TELEVISION.

Pinball, for example. With a decision by the U.S. Supreme Court itself upholding Portland's law banning pinball machines, passed during the Dorothy McCullough Lee years, Stan Terry has begun to collect signatures for a citizen's initiative to make them legal again. Passions are high.

And of course there's the Fong case, the albatross that Bill Langley hung around his own neck while running for district attorney. If elected, he said, his first order of business would be to obtain the indictment of Wayne and Sherry Fong for the murder of Diane Hank. And sure enough, little more than two weeks after he was in office, the Fongs were indicted.

Their trial—it would be the first of four, or perhaps five, depending on how you count—began that April, with the prosecution charging that Diane had somehow been poisoned when the Fongs switched the contents of a prescription medicine that Diane was taking at the time. As for a motive, the prosecution alleged that Diane had to be killed because she "knew too much" about Fong's nefarious activities.

Shockingly, one of Diane's girlfriends testified that Diane had confided to her that she had actually smoked marijuana with the Fongs. At the time, marijuana was thought to be something used only by blacks and Hispanics.

121

Things got even seamier. A police undercover agent, working as a bartender, told how he'd picked up Sherry one night and taken her to the Midget Motel on the outskirts of town, where, with police officers lurking outside the window of their cabin, she'd asked him to run away with her. Not until he knew the full circumstances of Diane Hank's death, he had told her.

> A POLICE UNDERCOVER AGENT TOLD HOW SHE'D ASKED HIM TO RUN AWAY WITH HER. NOT UNTIL HE KNEW THE FULL CIRCUMSTANCES OF DIANE HANK'S DEATH,

Well, she said, she'd come downstairs the morning after the party at her house and found Diane dead of an overdose of sleeping pills. Blood was coming out of her mouth and nose.

Then why, asked the undercover agent, had she wrapped the body in a blanket and thrown it alongside a country road in Washington?

"To fool the cops," said Sherry.

It didn't sound much like murder. But that didn't seem to be the point, what with all that marijuana smoking and carrying on in motels. In point of fact, it was probably exactly what happened—but the jury had had enough.

It returned after just three hours of deliberations, finding both Wayne and Sherry Fong guilty of first-degree murder. Then, less than a month later, the judge threw out the convictions, saying that the state's evidence was insufficient, and that the jury had failed to give adequate consideration to the evidence.

Much as he might have wished to, the new district attorney could hardly drop the case. A second trial for Wayne Fong—who now wished to be tried separately—was scheduled for October.

PINBALL MACHINES, the root of all evil.

The Black Widow Had a Slave

AND HOW CAN WE FORGET the lurid case of Marjorie Smith, the northeast Portland housewife, on trial for plotting with the family handyman to plant a bomb in her husband's car?

It was all over the front pages when thirty-four-year-old lawyer and champion amateur golfer Kermit Smith slid behind the wheel of his car, turned the key in the ignition, and was blown to bits when the car, wired with ten sticks of dynamite, exploded in the parking lot of the Columbia Edgewater Country Club.

Two days later, the Smiths' handyman, Victor Wolf, who, it developed, had a certain talent for things electrical, confessed, describing in great detail how he and Smith's widow, Marjorie, had plotted the murder. The plan, he told police, was for him and Marjorie—who, all commentators agreed, was a fine-looking woman—to move together to Alaska, using the proceeds from Smith's insurance.

> SMITH TOLD POLICE HOW HE AND SMITH'S WIDOW, WHO, ALL COMMENTATORS AGREED, WAS A FINE-LOOKING WOMAN—HAD PLOTTED THE MURDER.

Their first plan was for Wolf, a forty-five-year-old sad sack of a guy, to shoot Smith. As Wolf told the police, Marjorie, who had expressed her love for him in a physical manner on several occasions, even gave Wolf a gun to do it with. But when the husband drove up that night after attending a stag party at the country club, Wolf just didn't have the heart to pull the trigger, and ran away.

So they settled on the car bomb scheme. While Wolf placed the dynamite in the car, which was parked in the garage, Marjorie had coffee with the next-door neighbor in order to keep her from looking out the window. Wolf then followed Smith to the country club, and made the final hookup in the parking lot.

Marjorie denied any connection with the dreadful murder. In the strongest possible terms, she stated that Wolf was also lying about any

MARJORIE SMITH, "The Black Widow," claims innocence.

supposed sexual relationship. "Why that repulsive old man," she said. "Me be intimate with him? Never!"

The press called her the "black widow" and Wolf her "love slave"—which is perhaps why Marjorie's high-priced attorney, Bruce Spaulding, got a change of venue to neighboring Yamhill County, where, he reasoned, she could get a fair trial, despite Wolf's damning testimony and what one commentator has called Mrs. Smith's "complex marital history." Kermit Smith, as it turned out, was her third husband. However, shortly after they were married, she had left him to rejoin her second husband, who had also remarried. It was better than a daytime soap opera.

> "WHY THAT REPULSIVE OLD MAN," SHE SAID. "ME BE INTIMATE WITH HIM? NEVER!" THE PRESS CALLED HER THE BLACK WIDOW AND WOLF HER LOVE SLAVE.

The jury, which obviously couldn't believe that the prim and attractive lady before them—Marjorie wore a hat and gloves in court—was capable of such a heinous act, found her not guilty. One month later, Victor Wolf appeared in court to be sentenced for the car bombing. *Journal* reporter Doug Baker covered the hearing:

"The confessed slayer described the night in January when he said Mrs. Smith first suggested over a game of Scrabble that Kermit was 'worth more dead than alive.'" Wolf said he was 'surprised' and told her he would have nothing to do with murder. He said she told him to think it over, and she would talk to him about it again the next day.

"Wolf said on the following day Mrs. Smith called him to her bedroom. He said she was in bed, wearing nothing but a white chenille bathrobe. She asked him to sit on the edge of the bed and once again asked him if he had thought over her proposition concerning Kermit.

"'I told her I wasn't interested,' said Wolf. 'She asked me to kiss her. I kissed her and then kissed her some more. She put her arms around me and hugged me. We made love for a little while and then I went up and fixed dinner. . . . I was convinced for the first time that she was in love with me and I told her I would go ahead with the deal if she went along with it.'"

Princess Nena Takes It Off

BUT WITH THE BENEFIT of nearly fifty years' hindsight, it's clear that of all the momentous issues confronting the citizens of that time, none was more vital to the public weal than some extremely shocking developments down at the Star, the burlesque theater at Sixth and Burnside.

In the fall of 1955, the city council was meeting in special session to consider what to do about it all. To be perfectly frank, it seems that the girls down there had been taking off their clothes. And not just some of them, either. No wonder the town was in such an uproar.

> TO BE PERFECTLY FRANK, IT SEEMS THAT THE GIRLS DOWN THERE HAD BEEN TAKING OFF THEIR CLOTHES. AND NOT JUST SOME OF THEM, EITHER.

And it all went back to that fateful evening, more than a year earlier, when, following a high-speed chase on McLoughlin Boulevard, the cops had stopped a scantily clad Candy Renee and her boyfriend with a quantity of illegal drugs and a loaded revolver on the seat between them. As already noted, not even Candy's friendship with Diamond Jim Purcell could save her then, and she was forced to leave town.

The ownership of the Star then passed to a fifty-one-year-old accountant by the name of John Newton, who had somehow ended up holding a note on the theater. For a while he tried to manage it by himself, but it was too much for him—especially when the girls started taking off all their clothes on stage. Apparently the chief offender was a young twitch named Princess Nena, who wore an Indian headdress and, according to the advertisements, did "tribal" as well as exotic dances.

Herbie Hall was eighteen when he got his first job playing piano at the Star in the spring of 1954. So he was there for the sad end of the Candy Renee regime as well as the bacchanalia that followed. "It was wild!" says Hall, who clearly wasn't so busy playing piano that he couldn't look up once in a while. The house was packed every night. Guys were lined up outside the theater, waiting to get in.

PRINCESS NENA in working clothes.

INDIAN DANCERS at the Star.

Naturally, such goings-on did not escape the hawklike gaze of the local press. After the shocking rumors first surfaced in one of its

THE STAR, still open for business in 1954.

entertainment columns, the paper sent in cub reporter Gerry Pratt, undercover, who reported back that "the entertainment was pretty much nature-in-the-raw, and that some of the dances were considerably more than just suggestive."

Chief of Police Jim Purcell, first quoted as being surprised to hear that performances at the Star had been "out of line," followed up the next day by asking the city council to revoke the Star's license. The city council was convened to hear John Newton, the owner of the Star, show cause why it shouldn't do just that.

The city's star witness, no pun intended, cub reporter Pratt, took the stand, to be questioned by deputy district attorney D. H. Breuer:

> **Breuer:** Can you describe to the Council here the nature of the performance that you witnessed?
> **Pratt:** The program began with a review type of show. Four or five girls came out on the stage in cowboy uniforms and shot cap pistols. The show became extremely lewd when they went into the single act routine. That is when the girls stripped to—they stripped . . .
> **Breuer:** Then they removed all their clothing?
> **Pratt:** Yes. . . .
> **Breuer:** What was the type of performance which was given while the entertainer was nude?
> **Pratt:** She bounced around—it was a very small stage—she bounced around from side to side. There was very sensuous sounding music. She would do things like clutch the curtain. It was a pretty animal type show. I don't like to go into details like that.

Newton's lawyer tried to argue it was all just an illusion created by the theater's lighting, but to no avail. The city council, not fooled for a moment by such transparent pettifoggery, voted 5-0 to revoke the license.

The Star was closed.

is for music as th
box in the main ga
Possibly a police
Childers informed m
second room is for
only want to drink
On leaving Chi
that Tom Johnson had
couple of years ag
his income tax, a
said that he sett
ment of $60,000.

known operating the
e on N. Wms betwe
Knott, the westsi
et. Place is ups
e of the block.
tition to obtain
is place, this d
Childer

JACK F OLSEN
11 16 53

Friday
December 2,
4:00pm

On Thursday, 12/1/55, worked
trict #33 with Paul V. Font
#567.

This night can be recalled
that officer as at 12:30am,
day, 12/2/55 while southbou
N.E. Union Avenue from Knot
requested the Radio Divisi
give us a rolling check on
Oldsmobile, red and white
Minnesota license #EM 8269
incident will be recalled
were never informed by Rad
to the information on the

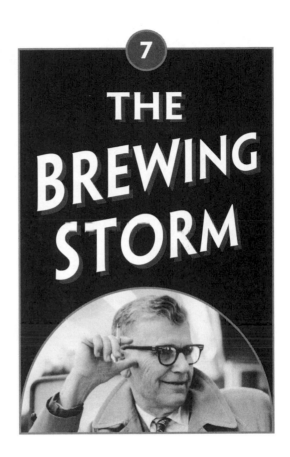

Our Man on the Avenue

WE should count ourselves lucky that police officer Jack Olsen has appeared on the scene: young, good-looking and, let's be honest, just a tad naive. But if that weren't so, there's no way he would have gotten involved in this half-baked scheme to expose the city's payoff system, one ten- or twenty-dollar bill at a time.

For starters, there is absolutely no guarantee that he will succeed in this endeavor. In this life, the odds against good winning out are always pretty high. In the city of Portland, in the late fall of 1955, they were probably more formidable than usual. But at least we now have someone in this story we can pull for.

THE PLAN, OF COURSE, IS THAT OLSEN WILL WORK HIS WAY UP TO THE BIG BOYS WHO ARE PULLING DOWN THE REALLY BIG BUCKS.

The plan, of course, is that he will keep a detailed record of all smile money given him in the course of his duties as a patrolman on the Avenue, gradually working his way up to the big boys—the precinct captains, the chief, the city councilmen—who are pulling down the really big bucks. And when he's got that nailed down, Jim Miller, the reporter over at the *Oregonian*, will write it up in his newspaper and expose the whole crooked mess.

When he gets home each morning after work, Olsen doesn't go to sleep until he's put everything down in his notebook:

We entered the East Precinct at approx. 12:45 a.m. Sergeants Moore and Sprague were at the front desk checking in the incoming officers. Sergeant Sprague told me at the time he would like to see me before I left. He stated approximately as follows: "I want to see you before you go." I replied by nodding my assent.

As we went to the front desk, Sergeant Sprague came to the door of the Lieutenant's office and motioned for me to enter. Sprague was standing in front of the first night relief's desk. He handed me a small, approximately 3-inch by 5 1/2-inch manila envelope. He said, "this is for that little deal down there." I nodded and put the envelope in my left front pocket.

I rode home that night with one of the second night officers in district car #24. On entering the house I went to my den and examined the contents of the envelope. In the envelope I found five apparently new Federal Reserve

Notes, all in $5 denominations. The serial numbers of the
notes are: L02020134, L02020136, L02020137, L81461003A,
L81461005A. Each note was initialed "JO" and dated 12-2-55.

The irony of all this is that Olsen really loves his job. He loves the
action, the camraderie. But most of all he loves the Avenue, the black
part of town that used to extend along Williams Avenue, from the
Steel Bridge to about Russell. He loves the sights and sounds of the
Avenue, the way the hookers tease him and call him "Pretty Jack."

There is one in particular, a young
prostitute by the name of Hazel Stamps. It
was never more than a friendship between
them, says Olsen later, but it was definitely
a friendship. Sometimes he would run into
her at the Keystone and they'd sit and talk.
Olsen, a graduate of Grant High School
and Lewis & Clark College, was touched

> OLSEN LOVES THE
> SIGHTS AND SOUNDS
> OF THE AVENUE,
> THE WAY THE HOOKERS
> TEASE HIM AND CALL
> HIM "PRETTY JACK."

by her vulnerability. She didn't know how to read. She could barely
write her name. "What else is she going to do?" he'd tell himself.

The Biggest Game in Town

AT THE TIME, the Avenue was a bustling neighborhood with nightclubs,
restaurants, rooming houses, and even a hotel or two. But the hub
around which everything seemed to revolve was the Keystone, owned
by Tom Johnson, at the corner of Williams and Cherry. On one side of
the building was a real estate office, on the other a diner that served
barbecue. That's where Olsen and Hazel would meet now and
then for a cup of coffee. At the rear of the diner was a door that
opened onto a gambling operation that did a reputed $100,000 in
business nightly.

Johnson ran the rackets along the Avenue under arrangements
similar to those obtained elsewhere in the city—with smile money for

the beat cops and more substantial payoffs for the ranking police officers and their superiors at city hall. But even if, by some magic, Olsen had succeeded in bridging the gap that separated him and his fellow officers from their bosses, he still wouldn't have been onto the biggest game in town—and, thus, on the Avenue. Then, as now, the biggest game in town is real estate.

IN THE SPRING OF 1954, the voters of Portland had approved an $8 million bond issue to build a new, deluxe sports arena, to be called the Memorial Coliseum. As 1955 neared an end, a battle was being waged over where it would be built—whether downtown, or at Delta Park on the floodplain north of town, or east of the Steel Bridge, in the heart of the Avenue. Fortunes would be made by those who guessed right—and as Jack Olsen went about his lonely business of writing down the serial numbers of $5 bills, men in higher places, with what they fervently hoped was inside knowledge, scrambled to buy up options on the property in question.

At the center of the scramble, of course, was Tom Johnson, who was not only the rackets boss on the Avenue, but its leading real estate practitioner as well. Old Tom, as they called him, must have known something. The old vice cop, who appears so frequently in this story, pointing us one direction or another, recalls how Johnson took him aside one day.

> "IF YOU GOT ANY MONEY," TOM JOHNSON TOLD THE OLD VICE COP, "YOU SHOULD BE BUYING PROPERTY OVER HERE."

"Sarge," he said, "if you got any money, you should be buying real estate over here"—meaning along the Avenue, down by the Steel Bridge. But on a salary of about $400 a month, there wasn't much the old vice cop could have bought, even if he'd been so inclined.

But you can bet that Jim Elkins was interested. He might even have thought he had some inside information from the local Teamster rep, Clyde Crosby, who sat on the city's Entertainment and Recreation Commission, which was studying the siting question. Maybe he did and maybe he didn't. At this point, nearly half a century later, we'll never know. But the point is that, even with everything about to come down around his ears—and believe me, it was—Elkins was still out there wheeling and dealing, trying to make a buck any way he could, and the more devious and underhanded the better.

So the stage is set. The final act of our drama is ready to begin. In a matter of weeks, the city will explode. All that's needed is a little spark. No way anyone could change it now, even if they wanted to.

> IN A MATTER OF WEEKS, THE CITY WILL EXPLODE. ALL THAT'S NEEDED IS A LITTLE SPARK. NO WAY ANYONE COULD CHANGE IT NOW, EVEN IF THEY WANTED TO.

What's Mickey Cohen Doing Here?

RIGHT IN THE MIDDLE of all this, celebrity mobster Mickey Cohen comes to town and takes a room at the Benson Hotel. What, you might well ask, is going on here?

If you've been following the story at all carefully, you know that he's hardly appeared in this little drama so far—and then with just a passing reference to his role as a strong-arm man for Bugsy Siegel back in the early forties. But he's a player. Old-time hoods will tell you that Cohen was a fairly regular visitor to Portland. Usually when he was here he'd meet up with Jim Elkins.

At least since the war, the syndicate's been selling brown Mexican heroin up and down the West Coast. It runs a string of high-class hookers through the Three Star, out on Barbur Boulevard. And let's not forget about the slots and money-laundering. So it's not like Cohen doesn't have business to attend to in the Rose City. The question is, why now?

We've already seen the deference shown the Lansky syndicate, not just by local mobsters, but by the Teamsters as well. If Jim Elkins or Stan Terry want an audience with a Brewster, they first have to go to Las Vegas. Then the pit boss at the Lansky-controlled Flamingo walks them up to Seattle. Lansky, Siegel, Cohen—it's clear as the pinky ring on your finger. For all his clowning and mugging for the press, Mickey Cohen is definitely big time.

Back in the early forties, with the race wire mission successfully completed, Siegel and Cohen were free to attend to the next items on the syndicate's agenda. For Siegel, that meant going to Las Vegas to start the Flamingo—the first major step in the transformation of a once-sleepy desert town into an international city dedicated to the laundering and skimming of mob money.

When Bugsy Siegel was caught embezzling from the Flamingo, he was shot dead. Cohen was left as the syndicate's top guy in L.A., which is ruled—rather inefficiently, by Meyer Lansky's standards—by an old-time Italian mobster named Jack Dragna.

Not surprisingly, Dragna was not pleased to have Cohen and his thugs raiding his operations and beating up his people. Cohen made the papers when a bullet from a .306 passed through his arm. Another time, they bombed his house, blowing up his wife's wardrobe and scaring his pug, also named Mickey, half to death.

THE PAPERS LIKED HIM BECAUSE HE WAS A SHARP DRESSER. THEY TOOK NOTE WHEN HE STEPPED OUT IN PUBLIC WITH STRIPPERS TEMPEST STORM AND CANDY BARR.

As Mickey continued to sell brown heroin up and down the West Coast, the papers continued to find him good copy. They liked him because he was a sharp dresser. They took note when he stepped out in public with strippers Tempest Storm and Candy Barr.

One of his business fronts was a haberdashery, but that didn't fool the IRS. In 1952, Cohen was convicted of income tax evasion and sent to McNeil Island.

After two years and three months, on October 8, 1955, he's out—and his first stop is Portland. In his autobiography, Cohen says that he intended to go to Seattle first, but the cops there wouldn't let him. So he settled on Portland. Besides, he says, "I gotta see somebody that's in slot machines in Portland, Oregon, anyway." He doesn't name

MICKEY COHEN, celebrity mobster from L.A.

him—or more importantly, say what he had to meet with him about. He leaves it at that.

With a small entourage, Cohen takes a room at the Benson. Everybody knows he's there. Of course, the cops are watching. The press has him staked out, too.

After three days, the cops—who, let's not forget, are working for Elkins—escort Mickey Cohen to the airport. Not, however, before he's had a chance to meet with the slot machine guy, who is, of course—no secrets here—Lester Beckman.

Whatever they had to talk about, Elkins knows it's not good news for him.

ANOTHER RAINY DAY IN PORTLAND

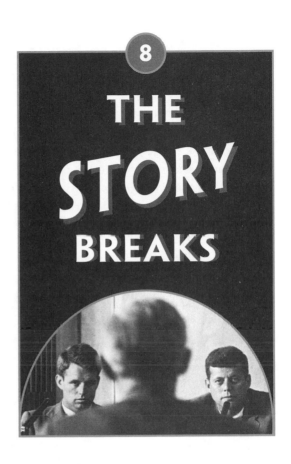

8

THE STORY BREAKS

Wally Turner Makes a Call

IT was raining that March day in 1956, so it's easy to picture crime boss Jim Elkins standing at the window of his office on Southwest Second, looking out over the river. And considering everything that had been going wrong for him lately, there's probably nothing he could see out there that made him feel any better, either.

We've been pretty hard on Elkins so far

141

in this story: called him all manner of names—pimp, dope pusher, armed robber, to list just a few—and pointed to a number of serious character flaws. But let's face it, even sociopaths get the blues sometimes.

The office where he was standing—Service Machine Co., as it said on the door—had to remind him of better days. Time was, it was bustling with busy workers engaged in the repair and maintenance of slot and pinball machines. The machines are gone now. Stan Terry has them all. After the Teamsters pulled that double cross at the Mt. Hood Café, Elkins really had no choice but to sell out. He never should have trusted Maloney.

So he'd tried to hire some out-of-town boys, tough guys, just out

JIM ELKINS had the tapes.

of Walla Walla, to—how shall we say this delicately—repossess what was rightfully his. And it could have worked, too, if the damn fools hadn't gotten themselves caught holding up a Safeway in their spare time.

And then, as if it wasn't enough that he couldn't deliver the Teamsters, that big fat loudmouth, Blubber Maloney, had tried to set up the town behind his back. He'd caught Maloney and McLaughlin, and the district attorney, Langley, plotting against him. On tape, no less.

So of course he'd had Crisp and his boys run Maloney out of town. Scared the daylights out of him from what he'd heard—which, satisfying as it may have been at the time, didn't solve the basic problem.

WALLY TURNER knew what to do with them.

Because when you get right down to it, in this business, the single most important thing is to maintain a relationship of mutual trust with local law enforcement. Chief Purcell and Lieutenant Crisp, now those were men he could trust. Langley's problem was that he wouldn't stay bought.

More bad news for Elkins: Terry Schrunk, the popular sheriff of Multnomah County, is running for mayor, and he looks like a sure bet to beat Peterson. It's bad enough that the new DA is trying to send him up the river. But when Schrunk gets in there, first thing he'll do is appoint his own chief of police, who will then put his own boys on the vice squad. And when that happens, Elkins knows, his goose is cooked.

As Elkins stands there, looking out at the rain, his phone rings. It's Wallace Turner from the *Oregonian,* and he wants to get together so they can talk. Why, sure, says Elkins, I've always got time for you, Wally. Suddenly, the day seems a whole lot brighter.

Turner and Elkins know each other from way back. When Big Mike Elliott, Terry Schrunk's predecessor in the sheriff's office, was off traipsing around Lake Tahoe with two hookers, who was it that tipped Turner off? And there'd been others. You might say the two of them have an understanding. Elkins knows Turner can't be bought. Turner knows a good story when he sees it.

As usual, Elkins picks up Turner at the newspaper office at 1300 Southwest Broadway in his big blue Buick with the wire-spoke wheels. The two of them park a few blocks away. It's raining harder now, so they have to keep the windows up. Between Elkins's cigar smoke and Turner's cigarettes, as Turner recalls, it's getting pretty smoky inside.

Turner wants to know something about a fellow named Joe Dobbins, a minor candidate for mayor—whether he's got pinball connections or not. Elkins sets him at ease on the subject. He doesn't.

When he finishes writing, Turner notices for the first time that Elkins looks old and haggard. He asks him if he's been sick. No, says Elkins, but he's been having trouble with these damn Teamsters moving in, trying to take over everything. They've even got the DA in their pocket, and he can prove it. Turner asks him how. Elkins tells him about the tapes.

Extra! Extra! Read All About It!

On April 19, 1956, the *Oregonian* broke the first of several stories based on Elkins's revelations to Turner and his partner Bill Lambert, with a big banner headline across the front page:

City, County Control Sought By Gamblers

"Seattle gambling figures closely associated with certain top officials of the Teamsters union have been trying for the past 18 months to take over law enforcement policies in Portland in order to establish illegal enterprises here, an investigation by the *Oregonian* has established.

"The police and other officials stopped them. Peculiarly, the local underworld also fought them and was instrumental in halting their plans, at least temporarily.

"The plotters' attempt to 'set up the town' to control the rackets has failed, largely because of their inability to trust one another and because of police determination that no mob was to move into Portland."

IT WAS ALL PRETTY much on the money, except for the part about the determined effort of the local police to prevent a mob from moving into Portland. As Elkins, the police—and, quite possibly, even some of the more astute reporters and editors at the paper—must have known, Portland had been mobbed up for decades.

> AS ELKINS, THE POLICE, AND SOME OF THE MORE ASTUTE REPORTERS AND EDITORS AT THE PAPER HAD TO KNOW, PORTLAND HAD BEEN MOBBED UP FOR DECADES.

The newspaper story identified the plotters as Langley, McLaughlin, Maloney, and one James B. Elkins, who was modestly described as a "longtime operator of pinball machines and other fringe businesses in Portland." According to the article, Elkins had been a "reluctant partner" in the effort to take control of Portland's underworld:

"Personally opposed to engaging in the prostitution racket, he vehemently objected to the Seattle mob's plot to bring in two Tacoma procurers to operate four proposed houses of prostitution."

WITH THE ADVANTAGE of fifty years' hindsight, it's always easy to find fault. But if only for the record: The reason Elkins had balked when Maloney and McLauglin tried to set up a couple of houses in town was that he saw no reason to divvy up what he already owned or controlled.

And as far as his being personally opposed to prostitution—his previous two wives had been prostitutes, and the wife of his current right-hand man, Ray Clark, was one of Portland's leading madams.

The article concluded:

"Elkins told the group from the beginning that in his judgment such an operation would not be tolerated by Mayor Peterson nor by Peterson's appointee, Police Chief Jim Purcell Jr. Elkins flatly refused to have anything to do with opening bawdy houses.

"The *Oregonian*'s investigation proved Elkins was right. Purcell's police force stymied every attempt the Seattle-controlled combine made to open bawdy houses. Wherever the combine tried to gain a toehold, the police were on hand to circumvent them."

> THE REASON ELKINS BALKED AT SETTING UP BAWDY HOUSES IN TOWN WAS THAT HE SAW NO REASON TO DIVVY UP WHAT HE ALREADY OWNED OR CONTROLLED.

As Elkins could have told you himself, behind every cloud there really is a silver lining.

The Town's in a Tizzy

THE OREGONIAN'S REVELATION of an attempt by Seattle mobsters to "set up the town"—presented somehow without mentioning that the town had been "set up" for decades—was followed the next day by another blockbuster. According to Elkins, identified this time as a "Portland nightlife financier," the local Teamsters representative, Clyde Crosby, had been involved in a plot to buy up options on land where the new Memorial Coliseum was to be built.

As would be subsequently established, Crosby, who seems to have been one of the more innocent characters in this whole mess, hadn't actually engaged in land speculation. He had, however, approached the mayor of Portland at one point, asking him to remove Purcell as chief of police—a fact that the *Oregonian* apparently considered proof of Crosby's own corruption, rather than the other way around.

Crosby fired back in the *Journal*. Elkins, he said, was "wired in" to the police bureau, which allowed him to operate unmolested.

"Ridiculous!" retorted Chief Purcell. "Illegal operations in this city have dried up completely. All the men on the vice squad have informed me that there is nothing open, and they are good men."

District Attorney Bill Langley, obviously not one to sit idly by while the very foundations of democracy were under attack, announced that he would be opening an investigation into the disturbing matter.

> "RIDICULOUS!" RETORTED CHIEF PURCELL. "ILLEGAL OPERATIONS IN THIS CITY HAVE DRIED UP COMPLETELY. ALL THE MEN ON THE VICE SQUAD HAVE INFORMED ME THAT THERE IS NOTHING OPEN."

Under the circumstances, the state's attorney general, Robert Thornton, had no choice but to step in, ordering the State Police to take over the investigation. Grand juries were impaneled. And for at least the next two years, Portland was kept in a dither by new revelations, accurate and otherwise—and not just from the *Oregonian*, but from Portland's afternoon paper, the *Oregon Journal*, which countered immediately by allowing Langley to write a windy three-part front-page series on how he was being framed.

Perhaps more usefully, the *Journal* persisted in pointing out that "Big Jim" Elkins, as they called him at every opportunity, far from being a mere "nightlife financier," was actually a hardened ex-con with a long prison record.

As can be imagined, this caused a certain amount of consternation at the *Oregonian*—especially when young police reporter Jim Miller pushed to publish his story about Officer Jack Olsen's investigation and the meeting at which Elkins had threatened to kill Miller's children and leave him floating in the Willamette. However, as Miller's editors informed him at the time, the Teamster exposé, infused as it was with all sorts of national implications, took precedence over mere tales of police corruption.

CAUGHT ON TAPE, Langley, the DA, lashes out.

IT WAS A GRAND newspaper war, in the finest traditions of American journalism—and just how much of this was due to the fact that the *Oregonian*, which was Republican, supported the incumbent Fred Peterson in the upcoming mayoral election, and the *Journal*, which was Democrat, supported Schrunk, is perhaps open for debate.

It is worth noting, however, that on May 17, 1956, the eve of the primary election, there was a dramatic raid on the home of Elkins's lieutenant Ray Clark, at 2409 Southeast Main. A search warrant for the purpose, alleging the presence of pornographic pictures at Clark's house, was cooked up by Langley, who desperately needed a way to discredit Elkins, and a reporter for the *Journal* named Brad Williams. And although the sheriff's raiding party failed to find any indecent photos, it did come up with twenty-six slot machines, a stack of what were then known as "party records" and—surprise—a complete collection of the King Tower tapes.

The next day, as Portland voters headed to the polls, they were able to read all about it in the *Journal*:

County Police Swoop Down on Slots in City

And in case anyone missed the point, photos of the two leading candidates—Multnomah County Sheriff Schrunk and City of Portland Mayor Peterson—casting their ballots that very morning, were featured prominently on the front page. Schrunk, who probably would have done just fine without this last-minute effort on his behalf, finished ahead of Peterson, but shy of the majority he needed to avoid a runoff in the fall.

Everybody Had a Story

BY ORDER OF the attorney general himself, the investigation was conducted by the Oregon State Police, who, then as now, were probably more suited to chasing down speeding motorists than dissecting systematic institutional corruption. However, as the record of their investigation—preserved in the archives at the state capital—reveals, they didn't do a bad job of limning the essentials of Portland's vice culture. In fact, much of the story you're reading now was taken from their investigative reports.

The chief investigator was a tall, thin, chain-smoking officer, Captain Vayne Guardane, who dictated long memos on the progress of the investigation to date, while other officers ran around town, following leads and conducting interviews. Everybody, it seems, had a story to tell.

Guardane and his charges quickly identified the players in the Portland rackets setup, starting with the cab drivers who picked up customers and delivered them to approved gambling joints and houses of prostitution. The plan was obviously to get the cab drivers to roll over on the madams and card room operators, who would then be persuaded to testify against the police officers who collected the payoffs, and so on up the ladder. The stratagem failed, however, when someone let out the word that if the cabbies testified about delivering customers to houses of prostitution, they'd be prosecuted for income tax evasion on the money they received for performing said services.

Most of Portland's madams and card room operators simply left town. Those that stuck around didn't give investigators much more than the time of day. The same applies to police officers who were involved in the payoff system. The old vice cop, for example, who worked directly under Carl Crisp, told the State Police he didn't know what they were talking about.

Some of the best information came from disgruntled Portland police officers, such as the one who had known Chief of Police

Purcell for years and regarded him as "utterly dishonest." Guardane wrote: "He states ever since he has been with the Portland Police Department, there have been payoffs. But individuals in the rackets made their own arrangements with the police department, not with any subject like Elkins."

AS IS SO OFTEN THE CASE, SOME OF THE MORE INTERESTING STORIES HAD NOTHING AT ALL TO DO WITH THE SUPPOSED PURPOSE OF THE INVESTIGATION.

Portland's highest elected official, Fred Peterson, was interviewed as well. But as the report shows, investigators didn't get much out of him. "It would be impossible to summarize his explanation," concluded the interviewing officer, "as it was impossible to obtain a cogent answer from the mayor."

The State Police, who obviously considered this an opportunity to vindicate their former boss, Charles Pray, who'd been driven out as chief of police under Dorothy McCullough Lee, zeroed in on Elkins, Purcell, and Crisp. While this could hardly have been what Elkins, or for that matter, the *Oregonian* had intended, Elkins's gamble in turning over the tapes wasn't an entire loss. Although the tapes were of limited evidentiary value—besides being almost inaudible, they'd been edited by Elkins and his lieutenant, Ray Clark—Langley was a sitting duck.

As is so often the case, some of the more interesting stories had nothing at all to do with the supposed purpose of the investigation.

Retired FBI agent Kelly Deaderick took it upon himself to inform the investigators of an incident involving then-Sheriff Schrunk one night at the Multnomah County Courthouse.

"The night watchman," the report explained, "had found the vault door ajar and summoned two cars of deputies to investigate. One of the deputies, finding the sheriff's office locked, declared 'Whoever is in there come out or we will shoot the lock off.'

"The sheriff then opened the door, and standing in his underwear, flourishing a revolver, retorted, 'Get the hell out of here or I will blow your asses off.'"

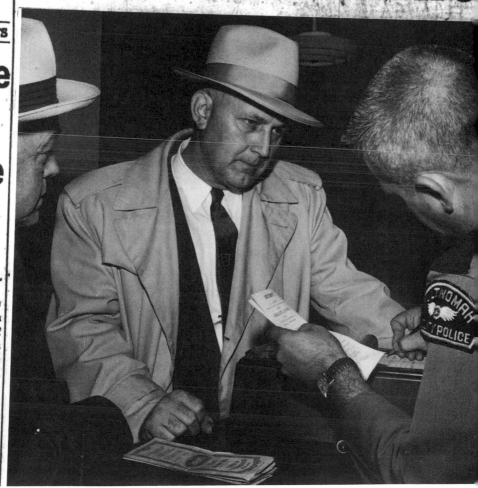

DIAMOND JIM wasn't used to this sort of attention.

Behind him, the deputies could see "his secretary in a state of undress" and "tax moneys from the vault stacked on the table for the obvious reason to impress his secretary."

Helpful to a fault, Deaderick also informed the investigators that "Schrunk had once been arrested by the Portland Police for adultery. That arrest," he said, "took place when officers answered a call on a peeping tom. When they arrived, they found a man peering into the window of a house, and when they questioned him he stated, sure, he was peeping in the window, but it was his own house and there was a man in the house in bed with his wife.

> SURE, HE WAS PEEPING IN THE WINDOW, BUT IT WAS HIS OWN HOUSE AND THERE WAS A MAN IN THE HOUSE IN BED WITH HIS WIFE.

"The officers and the complainant entered the house and placed this man under arrest, who turned out to be Sheriff Terry Schrunk. The records of this arrest, according to Deaderick, have disappeared."

Not so, says the old vice cop—who would have known, because he kept a copy of the records for himself. What had actually happened was that before the officers arrived at the U-shaped court apartments at about 42nd and Stark, the aggrieved husband had already gone inside, surprising the sheriff and his wife in the act.

Jumping out of bed, the sheriff had grabbed for his clothes and his gun belt, which he had left on the nightstand, somehow in the confusion discharging a round into the floor, then had run, still half-dressed, into the night before the police even arrived.

Always good to set the record straight, even at this late date, says the old vice cop, enjoying himself immensely.

Where Is Candy Renee?

RECORDS ALSO SHOW that the State Police investigators were fascinated by the case of the tantalizing Candy Renee. Well, who wouldn't be?

The same high-ranking officer who spoke to Captain Guardane about the utter dishonesty of Chief Purcell did not fail to bring up the matter of Miss Renee's arrest, following a high-speed chase on McLoughlin Boulevard, one fateful night in the spring of 1954. When he had noticed that Purcell was taking an unusual interest in the case, he had investigated further, to discover that Diamond Jim was a regular at the Star and had been seen visiting Miss Renee backstage. "This officer," noted Guardane, "does not know if he [Purcell] had a financial interest in the show or a personal interest in Candy Renee."

Investigators set out immediately to interview Candy Renee—the only problem being that since she'd skipped town, no one knew where to find her.

An early report showed that she had been observed in her act at the China Pheasant Night Club in Seattle. Candy, however, was long gone. Further information was received that she had been entertaining at the Rivoli, also in Seattle.

> INVESTIGATORS SET OUT IMMEDIATELY TO INTERVIEW CANDY RENEE—THE ONLY PROBLEM BEING THAT SINCE SHE'D SKIPPED TOWN, NO ONE KNEW WHERE TO FIND HER.

Two officers were dispatched to Seattle, where, according to their investigative report, "We made the evening show and a telephone contact with one of the girls and could gain no information on the subject."

Before leaving town, the officers also checked out several bars where, according to an informant, Candy had been spending a lot of time, drinking heavily and, if the truth be known, hustling the clientele. But Candy had apparently moved on. It was beginning to look like a dead end.

Then one July day in 1956, Captain Guardane picked up the *Oregon Journal* to see:

CANDY RUNS FOR OFFICE
Strip-Teaser has 'Fair Shake' Plank

SEATTLE, July 26 (UP) A shapely Seattle strip-tease artist filed for political office Wednesday because she wanted to see "everyone get a fair shake."

Candy Renee, auburn-haired headliner at the Rivoli theater, Seattle's only burlesque house, filed for election as precinct committeewoman from the 61st precinct on the Republican ticket. She formerly was with a Portland burlesque show.

Miss Renee said she is studying election laws and might also run as an independent candidate for the state legislature.

"I am deeply interested in wiping out the blue laws of 1909 that presently exist," Miss Renee declared. "I'm also against the state being in the liquor business. Washington operates controlled liquor stores. We must take these laws off the books."

Miss Renee entered the auditors office in a summer dress, but left when she saw photographers. She returned a few minutes later wearing a plunging V-neck dress "with nothing under it" and leopard skin sandals.

"Any man who can find fault with my platform is plainly closing his eyes to the facts," she said. "The voters will be seeing more of me."

"**LIEUTENANT HARRELL** and Sergeant D'Angelo will attempt to interview this woman while in Seattle," wrote Captain Guardane at the conclusion of his report.

CANDY RENEE registers as a candidate for Republican committeewoman.

OFFICER'S REPORT
OREGON STATE POLICE

No. ....

TIME ......1:45 P.M........

County ......Multnomah.......

Place ......Milwaukie........

...., 19......

Subject ......PROBE MULTNOMAH COUNTY

July 27   56

CANDY RENEE

On July 26, 1956, the following story appeared in the Oregon Journal:

CANDY RUNS FOR OFFICE
Strip-Teaser Has 'Fair Shake' Plank

SEATTLE, July 26 (UP) A shapely Seattle strip-tease artist filed for political office Wednesday because she wanted to see "everyone get a fair shake."

Candy Renee, auburn-haired headliner at the Rivoli theatre, Seattle's only burlesque house, filed for election as precinct committeewoman from the 61st precinct on the Republican ticket. She formerly was with a Portland burlesque show.

Miss Renee said she is studying election laws and might also run as an independent candidate for the state legislature.

"I am deeply interested in wiping out the blue laws of 1909 that presently exist," Miss Renee declared. "I'm also against the state being in the liquor business. Washington operates controlled liquor stores. We must take these laws off the books."

The 61st precinct, which Miss Renee wants to represent is part of Seattle's "skid road" area. It is bounded by 1st and 4th Avenues, Yesler Way and Cherry Street.

Miss Renee entered the auditors office in a summer dress, but left when she saw photographers. She returned a few minutes later wearing a plunging V-neck dress "with nothing under it" and leopard skin sandals.

She was accompanied by her attorney, Ned Cochrane, who said he is a Democrat. The 29 year old Boston born dancer said she knew her campaign would be "a long grind and a bumpy road," but she was confident of success.

"Any man who can find fault with my platform is plainly closing his eyes to the facts," she said. "The voters will be seeing more of me."

Lieutenant Harrell and Sergeant D'Angelo will attempt to interview this woman while in Seattle.

Vayne M. Gurdane

Vayne M. Gurdane, Captain

VMG:vmd

The next day, no doubt feeling the weight of the entire investigation on their shoulders, Harrell and D'Angelo met with the elusive Miss Renee at the Seattle Police Department.

"The writers," as police officers usually refer to themselves in reports, "questioned Renee about payoffs in the Portland area, and she stated at no time had she paid anyone while operating in the city of Portland. She said that while in Portland she fell madly in love with a Portland Police detective whose name she refused to reveal, stating that like any other woman she liked to be laid once in a while."

If the officers were expecting Candy to hand them the key that would unlock the Portland vice scandal, they must have come away disappointed.

The Whole Town's Going to Jail

AS ELKINS MUST HAVE HOPED when he turned the tapes over to Wally Turner, charges were brought against his erstwhile business associates, Maloney, McLaughlin, and Crosby, as well as a number of local coin machine operators. As he may not have anticipated, Elkins himself was indicted on nine state charges, ranging from bootlegging to accepting income from prostitutes. Elkins and his sidekick Clark were eventually indicted in federal court for wiretapping as well.

Seven lower-ranking police officers—all colleagues of Jack Olsen—were indicted for lying under oath about accepting bribes. As their commanding officer, Chief of Police Diamond Jim Purcell was charged with malfeasance in office for failing to prevent the acceptance of smile money. Shut down at the *Oregonian*, reporter Jim Miller—who by this time had been demoted to farm market writer— had told his story to the State Police.

> SEVEN LOWER-RANKING POLICE OFFICERS WERE INDICTED FOR LYING UNDER OATH ABOUT ACCEPTING BRIBES. DIAMOND JIM PURCELL WAS CHARGED WITH MALFEASANCE IN OFFICE.

To be sure, there wasn't really that much money involved. In approximately eight months of undercover work, Olsen had collected only $158.10. However, because of his meticulous documentation, prosecutors now felt they had proof that a payoff existed within the Portland Police Bureau.

With the indictments of the officers, the *Oregonian* decided it was finally time to run Miller's story—minus, as it turned out, any mention of his meeting with Elkins. After all, why go out of your way to damage the credibility of your star witness?

Bill Langley, the district attorney, was indicted on seven separate counts, including one for failing to prosecute a gambling operation at a charity event, sponsored by a local trade association, which he had attended at the Jack & Jill's restaurant. They had him dead to rights on that one. There was even a picture of him in front of a row of slot machines, which, we should not be surprised to know, Elkins had supplied for the event.

Even more shocking, the new mayor, Terry Schrunk—who by this time had handily defeated Peterson in the November runoff election—would be charged with taking a bribe while still the county sheriff. According to the story, first presented to State Police investigators by Elkins and Clark, Schrunk had picked up an envelope containing $500 by a water fountain in Kenton, a neighborhood in North Portland. The envelope, supposedly a payoff for not closing down the place, had allegedly been dropped there minutes earlier by the club's owner. Several city policemen, who happened to be lurking in the shadows at 3:00 A.M., said they saw Schrunk pick up an envelope. But of course only Schrunk and the club's owner—who, as luck would have it, was one of Elkins's boys—could have known what was in it.

> EVEN MORE SHOCKING, TERRY SCHRUNK WOULD BE CHARGED WITH TAKING A BRIBE WHILE STILL THE COUNTY SHERIFF.

Thornton, who everyone agrees was completely in over his head, did his best to stop the unseemly rush to judgment by publicly denouncing what he termed a "runaway grand jury," cutting off support for the two young prosecutors, Art Kaplan and Frank Wyckoff, who were conducting it. Kaplan recalls that Thornton wouldn't even give them office space. On his own, the new secretary of state, Mark Hatfield, gave them a room in a state building downtown. With no financial help from the attorney general's office, Wyckoff actually worked for free. Kaplan, who had been brought in from another state agency, still had a salary, but his wife had to type all their legal documents.

In all, three grand juries—the second of which had to be moved when it was discovered that Langley had bugged the jury room—returned 115 indictments. For a while it looked like the whole town was going to jail.

And then, just when it seemed that things couldn't get much wilder, Bobby Kennedy, who, as counsel for the Senate Rackets

regon Journal

DAILY WITH HER SHE FLIES OWN WINGS

Good Evening
Here is your
Family Newspaper

Home-Owned and Published in the Interests of the Northwest Country and Its People

N ·· 800 S. W. FRONT AVE. PORTLAND, OREGON, TUES., JULY 31, 1956 · Telephone CA 2-5511 34 PAGES PRICE 5c

Quits dlai

Chicago Polio Center 'Mobbed'

CHICAGO, July 31.—Anxious mothers and crying children milled and pushed at the doors of a polio inoculation center today as thousands of persons sought protection against an upsurge of the crippling disease.

Elkins, Eight Others Indicted by Vice Jury

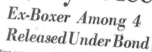

Ex-Boxer Among 4 Released Under Bond

Four persons, including Portland Vice Czar Jim Elkins, were free on bail today as police continued their search for persons named in indictments returned late Monday by the vice-probing county grand jury.

Arrested just before noon today was an ex-boxer, Joey P. Clemo, 28.

Monday night H. E. (Swede) Ferguson, 66, and Charles E. Canady (alias Chuck Brown), 29, surrendered to detectives along with "Big Jim" Elkins.

All four are accused of bootlegging in the misdemeanor indictments.

ELKINS faces 10 charges; the others face 2 each. Maximum penalty on each count is a six-month jail term or a $200 fine.

Five others were secretly indicted by the grand jury, but their names were not revealed pending their arrests. Today

For additional stories turn to Page 4, this section. More pictures

U. S. Grabs Egyptian, Suez Cash

LONDON, July 31.—The

Aluminum Deadline Postponed

NEW YORK, July 31.—Reynolds Metals company announced today that the Aluminum Workers International union in six cities covering 12 Reynolds plants had agreed to extensions of present contracts beyond the expiration of midnight tonight. A Reynolds spokesman said in New York the agreement involved plants in Richmond, Louisville, St. Louis, Sheffield, Ala.; Longview, Wash., and one plant in Corpus Christi, Tex.

Union and industry negotiators were meeting in New York and Pittsburgh today in

---

regon Journal

DAILY WITH HER SHE FLIES OWN WINGS

WATCH FOR
7-DAY TV LO
in your
SUNDAY JOUR

Home-Owned and Published in the Interests of the Northwest Country and Its People

N · 800 S. W. FRONT AVE. PORTLAND, OREGON, SAT., AUGUST 4, 1956 Telephone CA 2-5511 16 PAGES P

cell Indicted in Vice Prob

Mail Order Bride Arrives

MIAMI, Aug. 4.—A lonely, frustrated bridegroom-to-be nearly went wild before a crowd of 200 persons Friday when his mail order bride arrived from Australia.

There were sighs as lovesick Cecil charged to a fence to kiss Cecilia. It was obvious the crowd thought the two camels made the loveliest couple at Crandon Park zoo.

Discharge, Jail Meted To Marine

Jim Elk Faces N Charges

Police Chief Jim Pus was indicted Friday Multnomah county gra for "incompetency, n ance and delinquency fice," capping its nin vice and corruption prob surrendered and was re under $500 bail.

Also named in the fin of seven indictments ret by the crime-probing were James B. (Big Jim kins, a group of pinball ators, teamster union off and other patronan.

Elkins was accused of ing money from prosti and extortion. He wa

Committee, was about to embark on an investigation of labor racketeering by the Teamsters—showed up in town. And before you knew it, the whole lot of them—Elkins, Langley, Schrunk, Maloney, McLaughlin, Stan Terry, even Nate Zusman—got hauled back to Washington and put on national television.

▲ *PROSECUTOR ART KAPLAN* knew coin machines.

▶ *DIAMOND JIM PURCELL* leaves the courtroom in good spirits after the dismissal of all charges.

NATE ZUSMAN, self-termed "Mark of Stark Street," allowed himself to be photographed with lie detector equipment similar to that with which he took "lie test" at U. S. secret service headquarters after denying during testimony before senat had assured local m mind a quiet call ho trols of machine at t

stifies to Campaign Pressure

HE SAID he and Elkins then became partners in the Key Bridge club and the dance school, and used them alternately for gambling with cards and dice, and that this arrangement lasted until "October or November, 1955, when we closed down because

Maloney had left town the previous day after a breakup with Elkins. We decided to close because we felt we had no protection after Maloney left."

Ferguson said he once was told by Maloney that if he did not do what Plotkin wanted

done, "he would close

In early 1956, said, he and Elkins operations, again e Plotkin, because "we by hiring Plotkin we tection from the di torney and the union gang."

Big Jim Elkins Takes the Stand

IT WAS SHOW TIME. In late February 1957, everybody in town who had a TV set was glued to "the hearings" on Channel 8. Portland had three television stations by now, and as the local NBC affiliate, Channel 8 was able to provide an hour or more of coverage in the afternoon, live and direct from Washington, D.C. An expectant buzz rose from the galleries as the chairman turned to his counsel and instructed him to call the committee's star witness. Kennedy leaned forward, speaking directly into the mike with a nasal Boston accent.

> IN HIS ROLE AS STAR WITNESS, ELKINS WAS SUPERB. BY ALL ACCOUNTS, ELKINS AND KENNEDY, THE SON OF A BIG-TIME MOBSTER HIMSELF, GOT ALONG FAMOUSLY.

"Mr. James Elkins."

A kindly looking man with silver hair, wearing clear-rimmed glasses and a bow tie, took his place at the witness table.

"Do you solemnly swear that the evidence you shall give before this Senate select committee shall be the truth, the whole truth, and nothing but the truth, so help you God?" asked the chairman.

"I do. Yes, sir."

Now, that was a good one. In fact, there were places in Portland where this exchange probably caused a great deal of merriment.

"State your name, your place of residence, and your present business or occupation."

"I am fifty-six years old. I live in Portland, Oregon."

"Portland, Oregon?"

"That is correct."

"I believe," said the chairman dryly, "you can testify better if you get rid of your gum."

NATE ZUSMAN fails a lie detector test.

RACKETS COMMITTEE HEARINGS Committee counsel Bobby Kennedy and his brother,

Senator Jack Kennedy, question their star witness, Big Jim Elkins.

"Pardon me," said Jim Elkins, smiling sheepishly as he removed the gum from his mouth.

In his role as star witness, Elkins was superb. The fact that the Senate committee, like the *Oregonian*, wasn't the least bit interested in anything except the alleged attempt by Teamsters to set up Portland, certainly made his job much easier. By all accounts, Elkins and Kennedy, the son of a big-time mobster himself, got along famously.

Kennedy would later say that as far as he knew, Elkins always told him the truth. He couldn't have been that naive. In fact, considering his close personal friendship with William O. Douglas, it is highly unlikely that he didn't know the score when it came to the Portland underworld.

On the other hand, the hearings were, like any other congressional endeavor, highly political. Cynics will argue that the only reason the Democrat-controlled Rackets Committee was going after the Teamsters in the first place is that they had broken labor tradition by contributing to both parties. But whether the Rackets Committee was going after the Teamsters for this reason or another, it made political sense to accept Elkins's testimony at face value.

KENNEDY'S FIRST JOB WOULD BE TO ESTABLISH ELKINS'S CREDIBILITY: NO SMALL TASK, CONSIDERING THAT ELKINS HAD BEEN IN TROUBLE WITH THE LAW SINCE HE WAS A TEENAGER.

At the age of thirty-two, this would be Bobby Kennedy's first big job. Among the senators on the committee—officially known as the Senate Select Committee on Improper Activities in the Labor or Management Field—was his brother John, soon to declare himself a candidate for president. Others whose names still ring a bell these days were Barry Goldwater of Arizona, Sam Ervin of North Carolina, and Joe McCarthy, the old Red-hunter, now in political and personal decline. The committee chairman was John McClellan of Arkansas.

BIG JIM ELKINS slips out of court.

As counsel, Kennedy's first job would be to establish Elkins's credibility as a witness: no small task, considering that Elkins had been in trouble with the law since he was a teenager. Some of Elkins's early arrests—for vagrancy, auto theft, robbery, the sale of narcotics, and burglary—were apparently too small potatoes for Kennedy to concern himself with. However, there was really no way to avoid walking Elkins through the facts surrounding a conviction for armed robbery at a warehouse some fifteen years earlier in Arizona.

As Elkins explained it, a cop he thought he'd bought off had double-crossed him. And when Elkins and his partner broke into the warehouse, there was the law, waiting for them.

"And as you came in, he started to shoot at you," says Kennedy. "Is that right?"

"Well, I believed he was going to shoot the boy that was with me, but I shot back."

"You shot back?"

"Yes."

"Did you hit him?"

"Not bad, no."

More guffaws. This time from some of the senators themselves.

"Half-mast in Public Shame"

GETTING DOWN TO BUSINESS, Kennedy walked Elkins through the story about Nate Zusman's attempt to set up a whorehouse for Big Helen and Little Helen under the protection of the district attorney, Bill Langley—with the obvious intention of tying the whole sordid affair to Blubber Maloney, and then to the Teamsters leadership in Seattle.

Once again, Elkins stated that he had refused to help Maloney himself because of his personal opposition to prostitution. This was, as it should be abundantly clear by now, sheer nonsense. But you can understand why Elkins—a former pimp himself, whose previous two wives had been prostitutes, and who, as the fix in Portland, would

MAYOR TERRY SCHRUNK refused to answer questions on a lie detector test.

have had to approve all the houses of prostitution doing business in the city—might not have wanted to get into the subject.

Kennedy called Nate Zusman, proprietor of the Desert Room, where every night the town's pimps and madams hung out with the members of the vice squad, and attempted to quiz him on his role in setting up the house of prostitution. Zusman claimed he didn't know Big Helen and Little Helen were prostitutes. "Do I ask a woman who she is or what she is?" Then he proceeded to turn the hearings into a Groucho Marx routine.

> Kennedy: Tell me this: After Helen Hardy and Helen Smalley got this place on Pettygrove Street, did you ever go to their place?
> Zusman: I was there twice. . . . I delivered some sandwiches to them and I used to make barbeque sandwiches and barbeque spareribs there and we delivered sandwiches to them.
> Kennedy: Why did you do that?
> Zusman: I would do it for anybody.
> Kennedy: Anybody who wants sandwiches?
> Zusman: If they call the club, I will deliver.

BLUBBER MALONEY and Joe McLaughlin both took the Fifth Amendment on everything put to them. Teamsters officials Dave Beck and Frank Brewster claimed they hardly knew either Maloney or McLaughlin.

THE HEARINGS WERE GETTING GOOD PRESS. BESIDES, AS KENNEDY WAS AWARE, BIGGER GAME, JIMMY HOFFA, WAS WAITING IN THE WINGS.

And if, in the end, Kennedy didn't make an entirely convincing case that the Teamsters had made a determined effort to take over Portland, it probably didn't matter much because the hearings were getting such good press. Besides, as Kennedy was aware, bigger game—Jimmy Hoffa—was waiting in the wings. In his book *The Enemy Within*, Kennedy gives the Portland portion of the hearings hardly more than a footnote. This was just a warm-up for the main act.

For the good citizens of Portland, however, who were forced to watch their dirty laundry being paraded before the nation—on television no less—it was a deeply upsetting experience.

Portland's new mayor, Terry Schrunk, had started off well enough. However, when a disagreement arose over his testimony on the bribery allegations, he'd challenged the committee to give him a lie detector test. He took the test, but perhaps unwisely refused to answer several questions that he considered "loaded" or "irrelevant." For example:

While sheriff, did you receive any payoffs from bootleggers through Ray Kell?

And:

While sheriff, did you receive any payoffs from Stan Terry?"

Then Langley, the district attorney, was sworn in and proceeded to take the Fifth on virtually everything except his name and address. When one of the senators, Karl Mundt of South Dakota, attempted to get a straight answer from him, Langley, a fool to the end, attempted to lecture the senator on his oath to uphold the Constitution, of which, he pointed out, the Fifth Amendment was a part. "I am entitled to my legal rights," said Langley, "and you ought not to embarrass me about it."

Mundt exploded. "You embarrass yourself about it, and it is very embarrassing to me as a citizen of this country to find any district attorney presently sitting in that office, hiding behind the Fifth Amendment. It is embarrassing to me to think of the people of Portland, Oregon, with a mayor who flunks a lie-detector test and a district attorney hiding behind the Fifth Amendment.

PORTLAND'S NEW MAYOR DIDN'T TAKE THE FIFTH, BUT HE HAD PROBLEMS OF HIS OWN WITH A LIE DETECTOR TEST.

"If I lived there," continued Mundt, in words that would echo through the next few decades of Portland political life, "I would suggest they pull the flags down at half-mast in public shame."

It would have been embarrassing under any circumstances. But on national television?

HIKING COMPANIONS—Bobby Kennedy and Justice William O. Douglas.

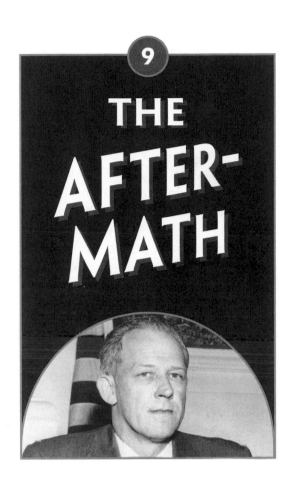

9

THE AFTER-MATH

A City on Trial, Sort of

WITH THE EMBARRASSING conclusion of the Senate Rackets Committee Hearings, the cast and crew of the Portland Vice Probe, as it was called in the newspaperese of the time, returned to Oregon. By the summer of 1957, a total of 115 indictments had been returned by three grand juries, and there were trials to be conducted. However, as any sensible person realized at the time, no serious effort could be made to prosecute the corrupt relationships so deeply embedded in both city and county governments without eventually sending half the population to jail, and certainly no one wanted to do that.

Tom Maloney, accused of conspiring with District Attorney Bill Langley to take over the rackets in town, was given a slap on the wrist and let go. Charges against Joe McLaughlin, indicted for the same offense, were dropped when Elkins—who, after all, had already taken him for $50,000—refused to testify.

Clyde Crosby, the local Teamsters representative, accused of using his position to buy up land for the new Memorial Coliseum, was found not guilty. At Crosby's trial, a psychiatrist testified that the state's star witness, Jim Elkins himself, was nothing less than a "criminal psychopath."

Bill Langley, indicted on six counts ranging from conspiracy to accepting a bribe, was tried first on the relatively minor offense of being present at the charity event where slot machines were being played. He was convicted on one count of malfeasance, fined $200, and dismissed from office.

Portland's new mayor, Terry Schrunk, accused of picking up a $500 bribe at one of Elkins's after-hours joints, was acquitted, largely because the jury couldn't believe that a public official of his stature would be dumb enough to pick up his own payoffs, especially one that small. They were probably right.

The trial was marked by the appearance of Bobby Kennedy, whom the prosecution had brought in as a character witness for Jim Elkins. After he was excused from the witness chair, Kennedy, who evidently saw this as an opportunity to signify his support of the entire proceedings, walked over and shook hands with the startled trial judge.

The outcome of the trial was probably never in doubt, however. As one of the jurors blurted out to Schrunk after the verdict was announced: "Terry, we were with you all the way!"

In July of 1957, Sgt. Robert Sprague, Jack Olsen's immediate

THE MAYOR, charged with accepting a bribe, goes on television.

superior at East Precinct, was put on trial for smile money payoffs. Olsen, a naive and idealistic young cop, had set out to document the payoff system that had existed in the city for decades, with the hopes of working his way up to the big boys in the Bureau and city hall. After eight months, all he'd collected was $158.10.

All his life, Olsen had wanted to be a policeman. And now, as one after another of his fellow officers, including the notoriously corrupt Lt. Crisp, took the stand to call him a liar, he knew he was watching his dreams go up in smoke. Years later, what he would remember most vividly about the trial would be climbing the courthouse fire escape every day, all the way up to the sixth-floor courtroom, in order not to run into any of his fellow officers in the hallways.

At his trial, defense attorneys for Sprague attacked Olsen's credibility by suggesting that he was carrying on an affair with Hazel Stamps, the young black hooker he had befriended on the Avenue. A picture of her, introduced into evidence, brought snickers from the galleries. As expected, the jury found Sprague not guilty. Charges against the other officers were dropped.

Chief of Police Diamond Jim Purcell, indicted on malfeasance charges connected to the Sprague case, avoided standing trial by resigning from office—thereby, in the opinion of the court, making the whole issue moot. Upon his resignation, he became commander of the St. John's district, where the shakedowns continued without missing a beat.

A laundry list of charges against Elkins was dismissed because of faulty indictments. The remaining charges against Langley were dropped for "lack of evidence"—although the state's attorney assigned to them says that Attorney General Thornton didn't bother to consult him before making the announcement.

Business as Usual, Once Again

AND BEFORE LONG, as the State Police reports indicate, everything was back to normal. The card rooms, the whorehouses, the after-hours clubs were all in operation as before—the only difference being that Jim Elkins was finished as the city's fix.

To be sure, Elkins hung on for a while, doing what he knew best. In 1959 he was caught sitting at the wheel of a panel truck in a Beaverton Safeway parking lot, while in the rear his trusty lieutenant Ray Clark peered through a telescope at the dial on the store's safe.

Elkins's old-time buddy Harry Huerth got busted as part of this conspiracy, too. In the end, Elkins got off because he blackmailed the judge, a homosexual known to take young men out of the county jail. Huerth, however, was left to cool his heels in prison.

In 1964 Elkins was rousted after giving some lip to a new vice detective by the name of Dick Bogle. The detective searched him and found an unmarked vial of pills that turned out to be methadone, a synthetic form of heroin. Elkins was convicted of possessing a dangerous narcotic, but his six-month sentence was thrown out when the state supreme court ruled that the search had been illegal.

> AND BEFORE LONG EVERYTHING WAS BACK TO NORMAL. THE CARD ROOMS, THE WHOREHOUSES, THE AFTER-HOURS CLUBS WERE ALL IN OPERATION AS BEFORE.

In July of 1968, Elkins was arrested again and charged with receiving stolen property. Police who raided his home at 11834 Southeast Powell found various items, including office machines, television sets, a motorcycle, and an outboard motor.

Three months later he was dead, under what anyone familiar with this story would call highly suspicious circumstances.

AS FOR THE OTHER principal characters in this long-ago drama: For the next three decades, Little Rusty continued to operate out of her house at First and Hooker, providing a place of refuge in her kitchen for the lost boys of the Portland Police Bureau to play cards at night. As, one by one, they grew old and died, she went to their funerals, not forgetting to pick up at each one of them the memorial cards once fashionable at Portland funeral homes.

Lonnie Logsdon, who ruled the slot machines in Clackamas County until put out of business by the massive State Police raids during the Dorothy McCullough Lee years, died in an automobile accident in 1964. Rusty would like to say that he was a "classy guy."

After her defeat for reelection, Dorothy "No Sin" Lee obtained an appointment as a member of the Subversive Control Board in Washington, D.C. She later returned to Portland, where she died in 1981 at the age of seventy-nine—very much alone, according to the old vice cop.

The fabulous Tempest Storm, now in her seventies, still performs occasionally at the Palm Springs Follies.

Candy Renee, the once-vibrant manager of the Star Theater who was forced to leave town after the police found drugs and a loaded gun in her car, tried once more, without success, to bring a burlesque show to Portland. She died in Seattle in 1993 at the age of seventy-seven.

Gerry Pratt, the cub reporter so shocked by goings-on at the Star, went on to become the *Oregonian*'s financial columnist, making friends with many millionaires and eventually becoming quite wealthy himself.

John Newton, the middle-aged accountant who lost his license to operate the Star after Princess Nena and the other girls started taking off all their clothes, ran off to Sacramento with Princess Nena, leaving his wife to file divorce papers in his absence. For all I know, he and the princess lived happily ever after.

Herbie Hall, who at the age of eighteen played piano in the pit at the Star, went on to perform in many other Portland nightclubs. You can catch him today, playing for shoppers at the Lloyd Center Nordstrom.

At the height of the vice scandal, Tom Johnson, who ran the rackets on the Avenue, left town to perform a similar function in Dallesport, on the Washington side of the Columbia River. By the time he returned to Portland—dying there in 1965 at the age of seventy-seven, law and custom had altered the strict racial segregation practices that had once enabled him to have such a hold on the real estate and vice markets in the black part of town.

His lieutenant, Birches Bird, took his talents to Reno. Before that, however, police sources say, he got involved with Stan Terry in shipping some slot machines to Ecuador.

Bill Hilliard, who, as a young boy was denied a paper route at the *Oregonian* because of his race, and as the editor of the tiny neighborhood newspaper the *Challenger* occasionally tried to call attention to the effects of vice on the black community, went on to become editor-in-chief of the *Oregonian,* retiring in 1994.

IN 1967, Stan Terry, who, following the Supreme Court's ruling in favor of Portland's pinball ban, had been forced into other illegal activities, fractured his skull in a fall from a ladder while painting his home in Lake Oswego. Upon recovering, he became a frequent candidate for political office, running at various times, quite unsuccessfully, for mayor, city commissioner, county commissioner, and governor.

For their series in the *Oregonian* exposing the efforts of the Seattle mobsters to set up Portland, Wally Turner and his partner Bill Lambert were awarded the Pulitzer Prize in 1957. Lambert went on to write for *Life Magazine*. Turner, who retired as West Coast bureau chief for the *New York Times,* lives in Seattle.

Fred Peterson, the druggist who served Portland as mayor during these turbulent times, died in 1985. His obituary in the *Oregonian* noted that he wished to be remembered as the "elephant mayor" because the zoo's elephant herd was started during his administration. Art Kaplan, the young prosecutor accused by Attorney General Thornton of conducting a "runaway grand jury," took a job, when his work for the state was done, as an investigator on the Senate Rackets Committee. Returning to Portland several years later, he attempted to set up a law practice but found that no one would rent him office space.

Bill Langley—the district attorney who was caught on tape attempting to divvy up the payoff with Seattle mobsters, but convicted only of failing to prosecute a charity gambling operation— returned to private practice after being removed from office. When he died in 1986, the head pro at the Portland Golf Club noted in his obituary that Langley, who "played almost every day for years" until the last few months before his death, "had a classic swing."

Also quoted in Langley's obituary was Robert Thornton. "In terms of the number of indictments, it was perhaps not successful," said Thornton, referring to the State Police investigation. "But when you consider what it did in cleaning up the city, it was a great success. Prostitution, gambling—those things were cleaned up."

For all anyone knows, Thornton may have actually believed what he said. Certainly, for almost fifty years now, that is what anyone of

influence in Portland would like you to believe. For his stewardship in time of need, Thornton was rewarded with an appointment to the State Supreme Court.

Harry Huerth, the old boxman whose recollections of Elkins's early days in Portland are so valuable, committed suicide in 1971. At the time, he was trying to go straight—attending the University of Washington in Seattle, and telling his life story to the eminent sociologist William Chambliss.

Wayne Fong, eventually acquitted along with his wife, Sherry, of murder charges in the death of Diane Hank, did not avoid prison. Sentenced in 1958 to ninety years in prison for the sale and distribution of heroin, he was killed in prison, fighting over a radio.

Mickey Cohen, remarkably enough, died a natural death in 1976, by which time he had served a second federal sentence for income tax evasion. According to the indictment, the plot to hide his assets had begun on precisely the day he arrived at the Benson Hotel after his release from McNeil Island.

Lester Beckman, the Portland slot machine king whom Cohen met during that visit, and Beckman's nephew, Ron Tonkin, were both called by the government to testify at Cohen's second tax evasion trial to explain some unrepaid "loans" they had given Cohen. Tonkin, who would become a highly successful used car dealer in Portland, says he went nightclubbing with Cohen in Los Angeles on several occasions. He says he found Cohen to be a nice guy, and had no idea that he might actually have had mob connections.

Supreme Court Justice William O. Douglas expired in 1979. At his side was his fourth wife, Cathy Heffernan Douglas, who was working as a waitress at the Three Star when Damon Trout introduced her to the justice in 1965. "I want you to always know," Douglas told her with his last words, "that no one has ever been better to me since my mother." As a recent biographer notes, Douglas, who disliked his mother, meant this as an inside joke.

RAY KELL was running things now.

tie temperature change.
Monday's temperatures — Maximum 8
degrees, minimum 56 degrees,

gman

4,600 Fans Squeal, Jum
s Elvis Shakes, Gyrates

here's no business like show business—and here is the most
enomenal aspect of it. This — as if you didn't know — is

Elvis, as he appeared to some 14,600 people Monday n
Multnomah stadium. The closed eyes mean he's "rea

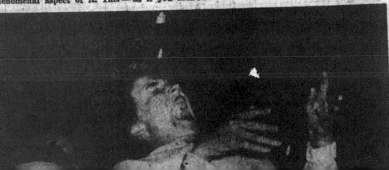

Stadium S
Of Bedlan

See Picture Page
All shook up?
That's putting it m
But there wasn't
mild about the reacti
14,600 fans who
touches Monday nigh
nomah stadium w
Presley took over.

Sammy Davis Jr., whom Justice Douglas and Little Rusty once watched at the Clover Club, went on from Portland to become an international celebrity—"Mr. Entertainment," as he would come to be known. He died in 1990 and was buried in Hollywood.

Nearly a decade after the Hoffa hearings, as they would come to be known, were over, Bobby Kennedy would return to Portland to campaign for president. Many attribute his loss in Oregon's Democratic primary, just days before his assassination in California in June of 1968, to the ill feelings engendered by the Rackets Committee investigation of Portland, particularly his treatment of Terry Schrunk, who was a bit of a hero.

Not quite three months after his overwhelming acquittal in court, Mayor Terry Schrunk personally welcomed Elvis Presley to town for the new rock 'n' roll sensation's first visit to Portland—an outdoor concert at Municipal Stadium. As reported in the Oregonian, the two of them were driven across the infield to the stage in a white Lincoln convertible, Schrunk in front and Elvis perched in back.

Schrunk would go on to serve three more terms as mayor of Portland, finally retiring in 1972 after sixteen years in office. Upon taking office he appointed his mentor, Ray Kell, head of Port of Portland and the E-R Commission, thereby giving him the reins of the city.

> MAYOR TERRY SCHRUNK PERSONALLY WELCOMED ELVIS PRESLEY TO TOWN FOR THE NEW ROCK 'N' ROLL SENSATION'S SHOW AT MUNICIPAL STADIUM.

Al Winter, who'd left town for Las Vegas during the "No Sin" Lee years, returned to Portland at the height of the vice scandal, opening a small card room called Dunkins Retreat, downtown at Sixth and Oak. He and a partner from Las Vegas bought two thousand acres on Sauvie Island, with the intention of building a casino and duck-hunting resort for high-rollers. Land records suggest that this was the same property that Bugsy Siegel and the mob had considered as a casino site back in 1943.

When Winter died in 1983, his widow, Babe, married her hairdresser.

AL WINTER, duck hunting on Sauvie Island.

Now ninety-nine years old and worth several million, she lives under his care in one of Al's old hunting shacks on Sauvie Island.

And finally, young Jack Olsen: ostracized by his fellow officers, he was assigned to work a graveyard shift in the records division. He used his spare time to good advantage, though, graduating from the Northwestern School of Law in 1964, at which time he resigned from the police bureau and took a job as a prosecutor for the Clackamas County DA's office. Five years ago, he retired as senior circuit court judge in Pendleton County.

One Last Good-bye

RUSTY REMEMBERS the last time she saw Jim Elkins. It was the fall of 1968, and he had stopped by the house on Hooker Street to tell her that he was going to Arizona. She remembers how hard it was for him to breathe. His emphysema was acting up, and he was wheezing. He asked her if she needed anything. Of course, she said no. But he asked to use the phone, anyway, and called someone named Florence.

"Now, Florence," he said, "you've got $250,000 of my money. If Rusty needs anything, give it to her." Then he showed her a snapshot of a roadside place he said he was going to open down there and he left. It didn't occur to her until several days later, after she heard about Elkins's death, that she had no idea who Florence was, and wouldn't have known how to get in touch with her if she'd wanted to.

The newspaper story out of Globe, Arizona, said that James Butler Elkins, sixty-seven, key figure in a Portland vice probe eleven years earlier, had died of head and chest injuries suffered in a traffic accident. The autopsy indicated that Elkins had suffered a heart attack shortly before his car crashed into a utility pole.

However, considering the fact that his body had been cremated the same day, the Portland police were naturally suspicious. So they sent someone down to Arizona to nose around a little. After about a week, he came back with a morgue photo of Elkins.

His gray hair looked a little curlier than usual, but it was Elkins, all right, lying there on the gurney. And if pictures count for anything, he'd died of a heart attack, too: two bullet holes in the chest.

MICKEY COHEN leaves the L.A. courthouse in chains.

THE MAIN PROBLEM for anyone writing about the Portland vice scandal of 1956–57 is that two of the major sources on it, the Pulitzer Prize-winning *Oregonian* series and the proceedings of the Senate Rackets Committee hearings, are occasionally quite misleading. In their eagerness to make a case against the Teamsters, both fall, hook, line and sinker for the clever cover story concocted for their benefit by Big Jim Elkins.

It's not that the Teamsters weren't bad guys, by any means, but their importance in what was basically a war for control of the Portland payoff has been greatly exaggerated. Ironically enough, a careful reading of the Senate hearings reveals what appears to be a decisive, behind-the-scenes role of a national crime syndicate in these events. Former state prosecutor Art Kaplan, who went on to work as an investigator for Bobby Kennedy on the Senate Rackets Committee, has told me he considers this a valuable new insight into these events.

For the most part, though, *Portland Confidential* is hardly an analytical work. It is simply an attempt to tell the story of a long-ago time and the—

quite literally—fabulous characters who played a part in it. Many of their stories come straight from the files of the State Police investigation, conducted at that time by order of the attorney general. Those files, now collected in several large cardboard boxes, can be found in the Oregon State Archives in Salem. Other stories were lifted from books, written by or about some of the principal characters in this drama, including Tempest Storm, Mickey Cohen, Sammy Davis Jr., William O. Douglas, Bobby Kennedy and, of all people, Harry Huerth, the old safecracker, or boxman, who knew Elkins in the early days.

It is Huerth's account (published under one of his aliases, Harry King) that puts the lie to so many of Elkins's claims to the *Oregonian* and the Senate Rackets committee. I would like to thank William Chambliss, who took down Huerth's story some years ago, for bringing it to my attention.

I am also indebted to all those who lived long enough to share their own experiences with me, including journalists Wally Turner, Bill Hilliard, Bud Crick; police officers Norm Reiter, Dave Bishop, Dick Bogle, John Roe, Bill Johnson, Frank Springer, Dave Anderson, Bill DeBellis, and Don DuPay; prosecutors Art Kaplan and Ralph Wyckoff; researchers Doug Neville and Sue Wunder; Herbie Hall, who played the piano at the Star, as well as numerous rounders who would probably rather not see their names in print. My special thanks to my friend Little Rusty, who had the house on Hooker Street, and to the old vice cop, who still doesn't want me to use his name. But if I tell you that during the time in question he worked directly under Diamond Jim Purcell and Carl Crisp, you might be able to figure it out for yourself.

Much of the material for this book originally appeared in the *Portland Tribune*. I'd like to thank *Tribune* publisher Dwight Jaynes for letting me write the original series and editor Roger Anthony for helping to get it in shape. Virginia Meyers and Tom Robinson provided invaluable help with the photo research as did Susan Seyl and Bob Kingston at the Oregon Historical Society research library. Thanks to Kathy Howard for patiently shepherding the book through production. To Tim Frew, my editor at Graphic Arts Center Publishing Company, goes the credit for coming up with the concept for this book—which, by the way, I hope you enjoyed as much as Little Rusty did. She says she's read it eleven times.

—Phil Stanford, *December 2004 (Second Printing)*

BIBLIOGRAPHY

The Growth of a City, E. Kimbark MacColl
The Shaping of a City, E. Kimbark MacColl
Rose City Justice, Fred Leeson
"Trouble in River City," (doctoral thesis), Joseph Samuel Uris

Shanghaiing Days, Richard H. Dillon
A Municipal Mother, Gloria E. Myers
20 Years a Soldier of Fortune, Floyd R. Marsh
Boxman, Harry King (Huerth)

The Money & the Power, Sally Denton & Roger Morris
The Mafia Encyclopedia, Carl Sifakis
Green Felt Jungle, Ed Reid & Ovid Demaris
On the Take, William J. Chambliss
The Lady is a Vamp, Tempest Storm
Fifties Flashback, Albert Drake
In My Own Words, Mickey Cohen
Sammy, Sammy Davis Jr. & Jane & Burt Boyar
Wild Bill, Bruce Allen Murphy
The Enemy Within, Robert F. Kennedy

PHOTO CREDITS

p. 3: © CORBIS; pp. 5, 78: Oregon Historical Society (OHS), #OrHi 91404; p. 6: Courtesy of historicphotoarchive.com; pp. 8, 43: Courtesy of Exotic World; p. 10: Oregon Historical Society, #OrHi 104167; p. 12: Al Mónner, Oregon Historical Society, #Al Monner – View 2; p. 13: Courtesy of the Oregonian; p. 14: Oregon Historical Society, #OrHi 73554; p. 16: Oregon Department of Corrections; p. 19: Courtesy of the Oregonian; p. 20: © Bettmann/CORBIS; pp. 22, 24: Courtesy of John Winter; pp. 24–30: Courtesy of Phil Stanford; pp. 32, 34: Oregon Historical Society, #CN 012108 & #OrHi 101737; p. 35: Courtesy of the Beckman family.; p. 37: Courtesy of Phil Stanford; p. 38: AP/WIDE WORLD PHOTOS; p. 39: John E. Reed/ MPTV.net; p. 40: Courtesy of Phil Stanford; p. 41: Courtesy of the Oregonian; p. 42: Al Monner, courtesy of historicphotoarchive.com; pp. 47, 48: Oregon Historical Society, #CN 013547 & #CN 013370; p. 50: Al Monner, Courtesy Portland Art Museum; pp. 53, 60: Oregon Historical Society, #OrHi 104165 & #OrHi 104179; p. 62: Courtesy of Phil Stanford; p. 63: Courtesy of historicphotoarchive.com; p. 65: Oregon Historical Society, #OrHi 105074; p. 68: Courtesy of Phil Stanford; p. 71: Courtesy of historicphotoarchive.com; p. 72: Oregon Historical Society, #OrHi 102235; p. 74: Courtesy of historicphotoarchive.com; p. 80: Courtesy of historicphotoarchive.com; p. 85: Courtesy of the McClendon family & Bob Dietsche. p. 86: Courtesy of Phil Stanford;

p. 88: Courtesy of William Hilliard; pp. 91–101, 122: Oregon Historical Society, #OrHi 104159, #OrHi 104175, #OrHi 104163, #OrHi 104176, #OrHi 104173, & #OrHi 104164; p. 103: NARA, Pacific Region SF; p. 105: historicphotoarchive.com; p. 106: historicphotoarchive.com; p. 111: Oregon Department of Corrections; p. 112: Courtesy of historicphotoarchive.com; p. 114: Al Monner; pp. 115, 129: Al Monner, Courtesy of historicphotoarchive.com; p. 116: Oregon Historical Society, #OrHi 104178; p. 119: Courtesy of the Portland Police Department; p. 125: Edmund Lee; p. 128: Oregon Historical Society, #OrHi 104162; p. 129: Al Monner Courtesy of historicphotoarchive.com; p. 130: Courtesy of historicphotoarchive.com; pp. 132–33: Courtesy of the Portland Police Department; pp. 133, 142: Oregon Historical Society, #CN 011013; p. 139: AP/WIDE WORLD PHOTOS; pp. 140, 143: Oregon Historical Society, #OrHi 83932 & #CN 018046; p. 145: Courtesy of the Oregonian; p. 149: Allan J. de Lay; p. 153: Courtesy of the Oregonian; p. 157: Courtesy of the Museum of History & Industry; p. 162: Hank Walker/Getty Images; p. 163: Oregon Historical Society, #OrHi 104170; p. 164: Courtesy of Zusman family; pp. 166–67: © CORBIS; p. 171: Oregon Historical Society, #CN 014684; p. 174: AP/WIDE WORLD PHOTOS; p. 177: Courtesy of historicphotoarchive.com; p. 182: Oregon Historical Society, #OrHi 105036; p. 184: Courtesy of historicphotoarchive.com; p. 186: Courtesy of John Winter; p. 188: AP/WIDE WORLD PHOTOS.

INDEX